P9-BBQ-337

English Grammar for Students of German

Cecile Zorach

University of Michigan

The Olivia and Hill Press, Inc.
P.O. Box 7396
Ann Arbor, Michigan 48107

English Grammar series
edited by Jacqueline Morton

English Grammar for Students of French
English Grammar for Students of Spanish
English Grammar for Students of German
English Grammar for Students of Italian
English Grammar for Students of Latin
English Grammar for Students of Russian (in preparation)

First printing December, 1980; second printing June 1981; third printing August 1982; fourth printing December 1983; fifth printing October 1984; sixth printing December 1985.

© 1980 by Brian N. and Jacqueline Morton

All rights reserved. No part of this work may be reproduced or transmitted in any form or by any means, electronic or mechanical, including photocopying and recording, or by any information storage retrieval system, without permission in writing from the publisher.

Printed in the U.S.A.

Library of Congress Catalog Card Number: 80-82773

ISBN 0-934034-02-8

<< Contents >>

<< Preface >>

English Grammar for Students of German is a simple handbook to aid students beginning the study of German. It is patterned after the popular *English Grammar for Students of French* by Jacqueline Morton and *English Grammar for Students of Spanish* by Emily Spinelli. It does not aim to replace the German textbook, but rather to supplement and enhance it.

Students of German often encounter in their classes and textbooks grammatical terms such as "direct object," "subordinate clause," and "relative pronoun," of which they have only a vague understanding. Using simple English and providing English examples, this manual clarifies grammatical terms by showing students how these grammatical concepts function in English and explaining how to apply them to German. It uses the conventional terminology still prevalent in German textbooks and makes no attempt to introduce any new linguistic categories.

English Grammar for Students of German assumes no knowledge of English grammar; it defines grammatical terms and concepts in ways particularly suited to students learning German. In order to simplify the presentation, exceptions to German grammatical principles as well as those points which have no English equivalents have been purposely omitted. The content and organization of the manual are based on a consensus of the material presented in beginning German textbooks. Thus it should help students (and their instructors) make the most efficient use of whatever textbook they are using.

Instructors who have used the two other handbooks in this series have found it most useful to assign specific sections as supplements to particular homework assignments or as reinforcement of grammatical explanations given in class.

I would like to thank my colleagues Prof. Robert Kyes and Ms. Charlotte Melin for their helpful comments on the manuscript.

Cecile Zorach

Ann Arbor
December 1980

<< Introduction >>

In order to learn a foreign language, in this case German, you must look at every word in three ways: you must be aware of each word's meaning, class, and use.

1. The **meaning** of the word–You learn new vocabulary in German by memorizing each new word and its English equivalent.

> The German word **Baum** has the same meaning as the English word *tree*.

Sometimes two words are the same or very similar in both English and German. These words are called **cognates**. They are especially easy to learn.

German	English
Haus	house
Garten	garden
Student	student
intelligent	intelligent

Sometimes knowing one German word will help you learn another.

> Knowing that **Kellner** is *waiter* should help you learn that **Kellnerin** is *waitress*; or knowing that **wohnen** means *to live* and that **Zimmer** means *room* should help you learn that **Wohnzimmer** means *living room*.

But generally there is little similarity between words, and knowing one German word will not help you learn another. Therefore, you must learn each vocabulary item separately.

> Knowing that **Mann** means *man* will not help you learn that **Frau** means *woman*.

Moreover, sometimes words in combination will take on a special meaning.

> The German word **stehen** means *to stand*; **Schlange** means primarily *snake*. But **Schlange stehen** means *to line up*.

Such an expression which has a meaning as a whole different from the combined meanings of the individual words in it is called an **idiom**. You will need to pay special attention to idioms in order to recognize them and use them correctly.

2. The **class** of a word—English and German words are classified according to **part of speech**. We shall consider eight different parts of speech:

noun	article
pronoun	adverb
verb	preposition
adjective	conjunction

Each part of speech has its own rules for use. You must learn to identify the part of speech to which a word belongs in order to choose the correct German equivalent and use it correctly in a sentence.

Look at the word ***that*** in the following sentences:

a. Have you read *that* newspaper?
b. He said *that* he was busy.
c. Here is the wall *that* he built.

The English word is the same in all three sentences, but in German three different words must be used because each *that* belongs to a different part of speech.[1]

---

[1]a. Adjective—see p. 116.
b. Subordinating conjunction—see p. 148.
c. Relative pronoun—see p. 105.

3. The **use** of the word–In addition to its class as a part of speech each word has a special function or use within a sentence. A noun or pronoun, for example, can be used as a subject, direct object, indirect object, or object of a preposition. Determining the function of the word will help you choose the correct German form and know what rules apply.

Look at the word ***her*** in the following sentences:

a. I don't know *her*.
b. Have you told *her* your story?

In English the word is the same, but in German the word for *her* will be different in each sentence because it has two different uses.[1]

NOTE: As a student of German you must learn to recognize parts of speech and determine the use of words within a sentence. This is essential because in German the use of words within a sentence influences the form of the words much more than in English.

Compare the following sentence in English and German.

The little blue ***book*** *is on the big old table.*

Das kleine blaue **Buch** ist auf dem großen alten **Tisch**.

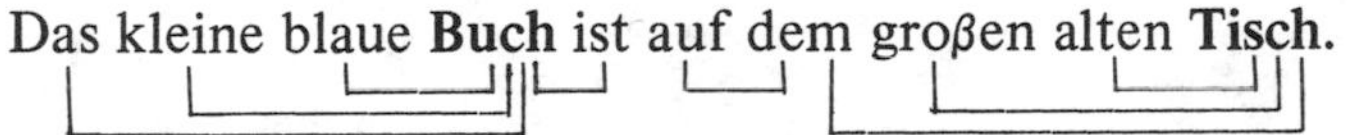

In English: The only word that affects the form of another word in the sentence is ***book***, which affects *is*. (If the word were *books, is* would be *are*.)

In German: The word for *book* **(Buch)** affects not only the word for *is* **(ist)** but also the spelling and pronunciation of the equivalent words for *the* **(das)**, *little* **(kleine)**, and *blue* **(blaue)**.

---

[1] a. Direct object–see p. 20.
b. Indirect object–see p. 21.

> The words for *is on* (**ist auf**) and *table* (**Tisch**) affect the spelling and pronunciation of the equivalent words for *the* (**dem**), *big* (**großen**), and *old* (**alten**).
>
> The only word which is not affected by the words surrounding it is the word for *on*, **auf**.

Since parts of speech and function are usually determined in the same way in English and German, this handbook will show you how to identify them in English. You will then learn to compare English and German constructions. This will give you a better understanding of the grammar explanations in your German textbook.

<< What is a Noun? >>

A **noun** is a word that names something:

- a person — John, Mr. Jones, teacher, sister, friend
- a place — city, state, country, Austria, New York
- a thing or animal — desk, house, water, dog, pig
- an idea or quality — justice, truth, peace, fear, pride

In English: Nouns that always begin with a capital letter, such as the names of people and places (Mary Smith, Switzerland), are called **proper nouns.** Nouns that do not begin with a capital letter (house, bicycle, piano) are called **common nouns.**

To help you learn to recognize nouns, here is a paragraph where the nouns are in italics:

> The ***United States*** imports many useful ***items*** from the German-speaking ***countries***. West German ***automobiles***, ranging from moderately-priced ***models*** to elegant luxury[1] ***cars***, enjoy great ***popularity*** with some ***Americans***. ***West Germany*** also supplies us with precision[1] ***tools***, ***cameras***, and optical ***equipment***. Many ***Americans*** are proud of their imported Swiss ***watches***. Nearly everyone in our ***country*** appreciates the fine ***taste*** of Swiss ***chocolate***. And some ***people*** here would feel lost in the ***winter*** without their ***pair*** of Austrian ***skis***.

In German: It is very easy to recognize nouns. German capitalizes <u>all</u> nouns, making no distinction between proper nouns and common nouns.

---

[1] These are examples of a noun used as an adjective, that is, to describe another noun. In German two or more such nouns are often combined into one, written as one word.

< < What are Indefinite and Definite Articles? > >

The **article** is a word which is placed before a noun to show if the noun refers to a particular person, thing, animal or object or if the noun refers to an unspecified person, thing, animal or object.

In English: A. **Indefinite Articles**

We use ***a*** or ***an*** before a noun when we are not speaking of a particular person, thing, animal or object. They are called indefinite articles.

I saw *a* boy in the street.
|
not a particular boy

I ate *an* apple.
|
not a particular apple

The indefinite article is used only with a singular noun; if the noun becomes plural, either the indefinite article is omitted or it is replaced by the word ***some***.

I saw boys in the street.
I saw *some* boys in the street.

I ate apples.
I ate *some* apples.

B. **Definite Articles**

We use ***the*** before a noun when we are speaking of a particular person, thing, animal or object. It is called the definite article.

I saw *the* boy you spoke to me about.
|
a particular boy

I ate *the* apple you gave me.
|
a particular apple

The definite article remains ***the*** when the noun becomes plural.

I saw *the* boys you spoke to me about.
I ate *the* apples you gave me.

In German: The article, definite or indefinite, has a much greater role than its English equivalent. It works hand in hand with the noun to which it belongs in that it matches the noun's gender and number:

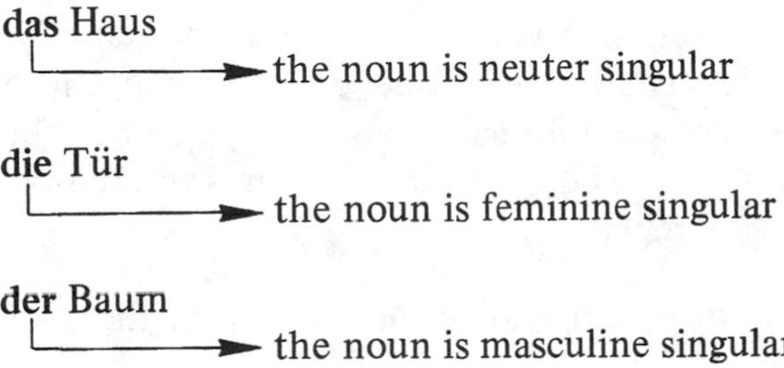

The article also shows the noun's case, that is, its function in the sentence (subject, direct object, indirect object, for example—see **What is Meant by Case?**, p. 11). In the three examples above, the articles show that **Haus** and **Tür** are either in the nominative or in the accusative case and that **Baum** is in the nominative case. The matching of the article and its noun is called **agreement**. (One says that the article *agrees* with the noun.)

<< What is Meant by Gender? >>

Gender is the classification of a word as **masculine, feminine** or **neuter**.

Gender plays a very small role in English; however, since it is at the very heart of the German language, let us see what evidence of gender we have in English.

In English: When we use a noun we often do not realize that it has a gender. But when we replace the noun with *he*, *she* or *it*, we choose only one of the three without hesitation because we automatically give a gender to the noun we are replacing. The gender corresponds to the sex of the person we are replacing.

The ***boy*** came home; ***he*** was tired, and I was glad to see ***him***.

A noun (*boy*) is of the **masculine gender** if *he* or *him* is used to substitute for it.

My ***aunt*** came for a visit; ***she*** is nice and I like ***her***.

A noun (*aunt*) is of the **feminine gender** if *she* or *her* is used to substitute for it.

There is a ***tree*** in front of the house. ***It*** is a maple.

A noun (*tree*) is of the **neuter gender** if *it* is substituted for it.[1]

In German: All nouns are either masculine, feminine, or neuter. This means that all objects, animals, and abstract ideas have a gender, as do the names of countries. Unlike in

---

[1] There are a few well-known exceptions, such as *ship*, which is referred to as *she*. It is custom, not logic, which decides.

The S/S United States sailed for Europe. She is a good ship.

English, where the few examples of gender are based on the sex of the noun, gender in German cannot be explained or figured out.

Examples of English nouns which have *masculine* equivalents in German:	Examples of English nouns which have *feminine* equivalents in German:	Examples of English nouns which have *neuter* equivalents in German:
table	lamp	window
heaven	fear	girl
tree	plant	grass
month	season	year
state	Switzerland	Germany
death	illness	property

You will have to memorize each noun with its gender. This gender is important not only for the noun itself, but also for the spelling and pronunciation of the words it influences.

Gender can sometimes be determined by looking at the ending of a noun. Consult the list on p. 159 for noun endings which often correspond to the masculine gender, others which often correspond to the feminine gender, and still others which often correspond to the neuter gender. You may find it helpful to familiarize yourself with these endings as you learn individual nouns in your German course.

<< What is Meant by Number? >>

Number is the designation of a word as singular or plural. When a word refers to one person or thing, it is said to be **singular**; when it refers to more than one, it is called **plural**.

Some nouns, called **collective nouns**, refer to a group of persons or things, but they are considered singular.

A football *team* has eleven players.
The *family* is well.
The *crowd* was under control.

In English: We indicate the plural of nouns in several ways:

- most commonly by adding an ***-s*** or ***-es*** to a singular noun

book → book*s*
kiss → kiss*es*

- sometimes by making a spelling change

man → m*en*
leaf → lea*ves*
child → child*ren*

A plural noun is usually spelled differently and sounds different from the singular.

In German: Nouns do not usually form the plural by adding *-s* or *-es*. Instead, there are several other ways of making a singular noun into a plural one. German plurals are less predictable than English ones; they are more like the *man/men* or *child/children* nouns in English.

Buch	→	Bücher	*book*	→	*books*
Wagen	→	Wagen	*car*	→	*cars*
Vater	→	Väter	*father*	→	*fathers*
Gast	→	Gäste	*guest*	→	*guests*
Frau	→	Frauen	*woman*	→	*women*

As you learn new nouns in German, you should memorize the plural form of each noun as you memorize the noun's singular form and gender. Consult the list on p.159 for some hints as to how different genders form their plural.

NOTE: Nouns do not change gender when they become plural.

<< What is Meant by Case? > >

Case is the signal for how certain words function within a sentence. The case of a word is shown either by the particular form of the word itself or by the form of the words which accompany it.

In English: The order of the words in the sentence signals the function of the nouns and hence shows the meaning of the whole sentence. We easily recognize the difference in meaning between the following two sentences purely on the basis of word order. The nouns themselves remain the same even though they serve different functions in the different sentences:

The girl gives the teacher the apple.

Here *the girl* is giving,
and *the teacher* is receiving.

The teacher gives the girl the apple.

Here *the teacher* is giving,
and *the girl* is receiving.

If we begin moving the words around, we can make up nonsense sentences like the following:

The apple is giving the teacher the girl.
The girl is giving the apple the teacher.

We understand these sentences, but they do not make much sense. We have completely changed the meaning of the sentence by changing the position of the three nouns in it.

We are aware of case in English only with pronouns. (See **What is a Personal Pronoun?**, p. 33.) In the two examples below, it is not just the word order but also the form, i.e. the case, of the pronoun which affects the sentence's meaning:

I know *them*.
They know *me*.

We cannot say, "I know *they*" or "They know *I*" because the forms "they" and "I" cannot be used as objects of a verb (see **What are Objects?**, p.20). If you can recognize the different cases of pronouns in English you may find it easier to understand the German case system.

English pronouns have three cases:

1. **nominative**: used for subjects and predicate nouns (see **What is a Subject?**, p. 18 and **What is a Predicate Noun?**, p. 26).

    He and *I* went to the movies.
    subjects = nominative case

    We enjoyed the film.
    subject = nominative case

2. **objective**: used for direct objects, indirect objects, and objects of prepositions (see **What are Objects?**, p. 20).

They invited both *him* and *me.*
subject = nominative case — direct objects = objective case

They sent *us* a note.
subject = nominative — indirect object = objective

We asked about *them.*
subject = nominative — object of preposition = objective

They spoke to *her.*
subject = nominative — object of preposition = objective

In these examples the pronouns have different forms depending on how they are used in the sentence. The different cases prevent us from saying "Us went to the movies" or "Him talked about she."

3. **possessive:** used to show ownership; the possessive pronoun can function as subject, predicate noun, direct object, indirect object, or object of preposition.

Is this book *yours*?
possessive pronoun = predicate noun

John called his parents, but I wrote *mine* a letter.
possessive pronoun = indirect object

Mary has finished her test, but John is still working on *his.*
possessive pronoun = object of preposition

The possessive case is discussed in a separate section (see **What is a Possessive Pronoun**?, p. 90).

In German: Word order does not show the function of nouns within a sentence. Instead, German uses a signal called **case.** The ending on the definite or indefinite article with each noun shows the noun's case (see **What are Indefinite and Definite Articles?**, p. 6). As long as the nouns are put in their proper cases, the words in the sentence can be moved around in a variety of ways without changing the essential meaning of the sentence.

Look at the many ways the following sentence can be expressed in German:

The girl gives the teacher the apple.

- Das Mädchen gibt dem Lehrer den Apfel.
  nominative — dative — accusative
  the girl gives to the teacher the apple

- Dem Lehrer gibt das Mädchen den Apfel.
  dative — nominative — accusative
  to the teacher gives the girl the apple

- Den Apfel gibt das Mädchen dem Lehrer.
  accusative — nominative — dative
  the apple gives the girl to the teacher

Because of the different case endings on the articles (**das, dem, den**, all meaning "the"), all three of these sentences show that *the girl* (**das Mädchen**-nominative-in all three sentences) is doing the giving and *the teacher* (**dem Lehrer**-dative-in all three sentences) is doing the receiving. The different word order in all three sentences simply shows what the writer of the sentence wants to stress.

German has four different cases for nouns:

1. the nominative
2. the genitive
3. the dative
4. the accusative

The complete set of case forms of any given noun (shown by the endings on the article which accompanies it) is called the noun's **declension**. When you have memorized these forms, you are able to "decline" that noun. The different cases are used as follows:

The **nominative case** is used for the *subject* of a sentence and for *predicate nouns* in the sentence. (See **What is a Subject?**, p. 18 and **What is a Predicate Noun?**, p. 26.)

The **genitive case** is used to show *possession*. (See **What is the Possessive?**, p. 28.)

The **dative case** is used for *indirect objects* and for direct objects of a few verbs. (See **What are Objects?**, p. 20.)

The **accusative case** is used for most *direct objects*.

The **accusative, dative**, and occasionally the **genitive** are used for *objects of a preposition*. (See **What is a Preposition?**, p. 130.)

Your German textbook will show you the case endings for the definite and indefinite articles; you will need to memorize these until they become automatic.

To show you how a change in case leads to a change in meaning, we have taken the sentence used above, "The girl is giving the teacher the apple," and by changing the case of the nouns in German we have changed the sentence to mean "The teacher is giving the girl the apple."

The teacher gives the girl the apple.

• Dem Mädchen	gibt	der Lehrer	den Apfel.
dative		nominative	accusative
to the girl	gives	the teacher	the apple
• Der Lehrer	gibt	dem Mädchen	den Apfel.
nominative		dative	accusative
the teacher	gives	to the girl	the apple
• Den Apfel	gibt	der Lehrer	dem Mädchen.
accusative		nominative	dative
the apple	gives	the teacher	to the girl

In deciding which case to use in a German sentence like the example you will need to go through a series of steps:

The teacher gives the girl the apple.

1. Identify the gender and number of each noun.

teacher[1]:	**Der Lehrer** is masculine singular.
girl:	**Das Mädchen** is neuter singular.
apple:	**Der Apfel** is masculine singular.

2. Determine how each noun functions in the sentence.

teacher	=	subject
girl	=	indirect object
apple	=	direct object

3. Determine what case in German corresponds to the function you have identified in step 2.

teacher	=	subject	→	nominative case
girl	=	indirect object	→	dative case
apple	=	direct object	→	accusative case

[1] In German there is also a feminine word for teacher if the teacher is a woman.

4. Choose the proper form from those which you have memorized.

Der Lehrer gibt dem Mädchen den Apfel.

Der Lehrer	dem Mädchen	den Apfel
masc. sing. nom.	neut. sing. dat.	masc. sing. acc.

Notice how changing the function of a word in a German sentence requires changing its case as well:

- *The girl knows the teacher.*
  Das Mädchen kennt **den** Lehrer.
  Das Mädchen: subject = nominative; den Lehrer: direct object = accusative

- *The teacher knows the girl.*
  Der Lehrer kennt das Mädchen.
  Der Lehrer: subject = nominative; das Mädchen: direct object = accusative

(The word **Mädchen** also has two different cases in the above two sentences, but they have identical forms and hence look alike.)

<< What is a Subject? >>

The **subject** of a sentence is the person or thing that performs the action. When you wish to find the subject of a sentence, look for the verb first; then ask, *who?* **or** *what?* **before the verb**. The answer will be the subject.

Peter studies German.

Who studies German?	Answer: Peter.
Peter is the subject.	(Singular subject)

Did Kathryn and Mary visit Dresden?

Who visited Dresden?	Answer: Kathryn and Mary.
Kathryn and Mary is the subject.	(Plural subject)

Train yourself always to ask the question to find the subject. Never assume that a word is the subject because it comes first in the sentence. Subjects can be in many different places of a sentence, as you can see in the following examples in which the subject is in boldface and the verb italicized:

After running 26 miles, ***Ann*** *was* very tired.
Standing at the top of the stairs *was* a tall ***man***.

Some sentences have more than one conjugated verb; you must find the subject of each verb.

The ***boys*** *were doing* the cooking while ***Mary*** *was setting* the table.

Boys is the plural subject of *were doing*.
Mary is the singular subject of *was setting*.

In English and in German it is very important to find the subject of each verb and to make sure that the subject and verb agree. You must choose the form of the verb which goes with the subject: if the subject is singular, the verb must be singular; if the subject is plural, the verb must be plural. (See **What is a Verb Conjugation?**, p. 50.)

In German: It is particularly important that you recognize the subject of a sentence so that you will put it in the proper case (see **What is Meant by Case?**, p. 11). The subject of a German sentence is in the nominative case.

- **Der Mann** singt laut.

  nominative 3rd person singular
  masc. singular

  ***The man** is singing loudly.*

- **Das Kind** spielt allein.

  nominative 3rd person singular
  neuter singular

  ***The child** is playing alone.*

- **Die Frau** arbeitet heute.

  nominative 3rd person singular
  fem. singular

  ***The woman** is working today.*

- **Wir** kommen spät.

  nominative 1st person plural
  1st person plural

  ***We** are coming late.*

< < What are Objects? > >

Every sentence consists, at the very least, of a subject and a verb:

Children play.
Work stopped.

The subject of the sentence is a noun or a pronoun. Most sentences, however, contain other nouns or pronouns. Many of the nouns or pronouns in a sentence function as **objects.** These objects are divided into three categories depending upon their position in the sentence and how they are used. The three types of objects are:

1. direct object
2. indirect object
3. object of a preposition

1. Direct object and 2. Indirect object

In English:

1. **Direct object**: It receives the action of the verb or shows the result of that action directly, without prepositions separating the verb from the receiver. It answers the **one-word question** *what?* **or** *whom?* **asked after the verb.**

- Paul reads ***the book***.

  Paul reads *what*? The book.
  The book is the direct object.

- They invite ***Paul and his sister***.

  They invite *whom*? Paul and his sister.
  Paul and his sister are the two direct objects.

Never assume that a word is the direct object. Always ask the one-word question and if you don't get an answer, you don't have a direct object in the sentence.

- John writes well.

  John writes *what*? No answer.
  John writes *whom*? No answer.

This sentence has no direct object. (*Well* is an adverb.)

2. **Indirect object**: It also receives the action of the verb or shows the result of that action. However, it receives the action indirectly; it explains "to whom," "to what," "for whom," or "for what" the action of the verb is done. It answers the **two-word question** *to whom/for whom* **or** *to what/for what* **asked after the verb**.

   - John writes ***his brother***.

     John writes *to whom*? To his brother.
     His brother is the indirect object.

   - Susan did ***me*** a favor.

     Susan did a favor *for whom*? For me.
     Me is the indirect object.

In German: Objects are divided into categories depending on their case, mainly accusative and dative. An object will never be in the nominative, and you will probably never encounter an object in the genitive.

1. **Direct object**: Most English direct objects are in the accusative case in German.

   - *Paul reads* ***the book***.

     Paul reads *what*? The book
     The book is the direct object.

   Paul liest **das Buch**.
   subject — neuter sing.
   direct object = accusative

- *They invite **Paul and his sister.***

  They invite *who(m)*? Paul and his sister.
  Paul and his sister is the direct object.

  Sie laden **Paul und seine Schwester** ein.
  subject — direct objects = accusative

A few common German verbs, however, require a dative object even though their English equivalents have direct objects. Your German textbook will tell you about these verbs, and you will need to memorize them. Here are two examples:

- *They thank **the policeman**.*

  They thank *who(m)*? The policeman.
  The policeman is the direct object.

  Sie danken **dem Polizisten.**
  subject — dative object

  The verb **danken** (*to thank*) requires a dative object.

- *We are helping **you**.*

  We are helping *who(m)*? You.
  You is the direct object.

  Wir helfen **dir**.
  subject — dative object

  The verb **helfen** (*to help*) requires a dative object.

2. **Indirect object**: Most English indirect objects are dative objects in German.

- *John writes **his brother**.*

  John writes *to whom*? His brother.
  His brother is the indirect object.

  John schreibt **seinem Bruder**.
  subject — dative object

- *Susan did **me** a favor.*

  Susan did a favor *for whom*? Me.
  Me is the indirect object.

  Susan tat **mir** einen Gefallen.
  subject dative object accusative object

A sentence may contain both a direct object and an indirect object.

In English: Many verbs in English have two objects. In the sentence the indirect object will usually come before the direct object.

- He bought his mother flowers.
  subject verb indirect object direct object

  He bought *what*? Flowers.
  Flowers is the direct object.

  He bought flowers *for whom*? For his mother.
  His mother is the indirect object.

- We gave the postman the letter.
  subject verb indirect object direct object

  We gave *what*? The letter.
  The letter is the direct object.

  We gave the letter *to whom*? To the postman.
  The postman is the indirect object.

In German: In a sentence with two objects you will need to determine which object is the direct object and which object is the indirect object. The direct object will be in the accusative case and the indirect object will be in the dative.

- *He bought **his mother flowers**.*

  subject — indirect object — direct object

  Er kaufte **seiner Mutter Blumen**.

  subject — dative object — accusative object

- *We gave **the postman the letter**.*

  subject — indirect object — direct object

  Wir gaben **dem Briefträger den Brief**.

  subject — dative object — accusative object

3. Object of a Preposition

In English: The noun or pronoun which follows the preposition is called the **object of the preposition**. The object of the preposition answers a **two-word question** made up of the **preposition** + *what* or *whom*.

- The book is ***in the desk***.

  The book is *in what*? In the desk.
  The desk is the object of the preposition *in*.

- John is leaving ***with Paul***.

  John is leaving *with whom*? With Paul.
  Paul is the object of the preposition *with*.

In German: Objects of a preposition are as easy to identify as they are in English. German prepositions, however, have objects in particular cases, usually accusative or dative, sometimes genitive (see **What is Meant by a Preposition?**, p. 130). As you memorize prepositions, you will need to learn the case which follows each preposition. For example, here are three different prepositions, each requiring a different case:

für diesen Mann — *for this man*
accusative with **für**

von solchen Büchern — *about such books*
dative with **von**

wegen des Sturmes — *on account of the storm*
genitive with **wegen**

As a student of German you must watch out for the following pitfalls:

1. An English verb that takes a preposition and object of a preposition may have a German equivalent which takes simply an accusative or a dative object:

    She is looking for ***her coat.***

    She is looking *for what*? Her coat.
    Her coat is the object of the preposition *for.*

    Sie sucht **ihren Mantel**.
    accusative object

    The verb **suchen** is the equivalent of *to look for* and takes an accusative object.

2. Sometimes an English verb that takes a preposition and object of a preposition may have a German equivalent which also takes a preposition and object of a preposition, but the German preposition will be different from the English one, having a completely different meaning.

    He is waiting ***for*** *his friend.*
    Er wartet **auf** seinen Freund.
    on

    I am asking you ***for*** *advice.*
    Ich bitte dich **um** Rat.
    about

You can avoid these pitfalls by learning German as a separate language with structures different from English and by avoiding the temptation to translate words, phrases, and sentences word-for-word from English into German. Your German textbook will introduce phrases like **warten auf** + accusative object (*to wait for*) and **bitten um** + accusative object (*to ask for*) for you to memorize. Make sure that you learn the whole pattern so that you will use it correctly.

<< What is a Predicate Noun? >>

A **predicate noun** in a sentence is a noun which points to the same thing as the sentence's subject and which is connected to the subject by a linking verb. A **linking verb** is a kind of intransitive verb (see p. 45) which *links* the subject to another word.

In English: Some common linking verbs in English are ***to be***, ***to seem***, ***to appear***, ***to become***. Although these verbs often have a noun after them in the sentence, this noun is not a direct object (see **What are Objects?**, p. 20); instead, it is called a predicate noun.

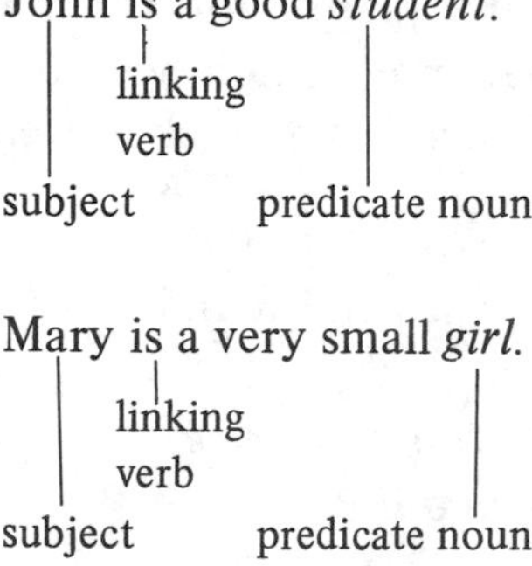

In German: Predicate nouns are in the nominative case (see **What is Meant by Case?**, p. 11). They point to the subject, which is also in the nominative case. Usually the noun itself does not show case. However, you must know its case in order to use the proper form of the article and adjectives preceding it.

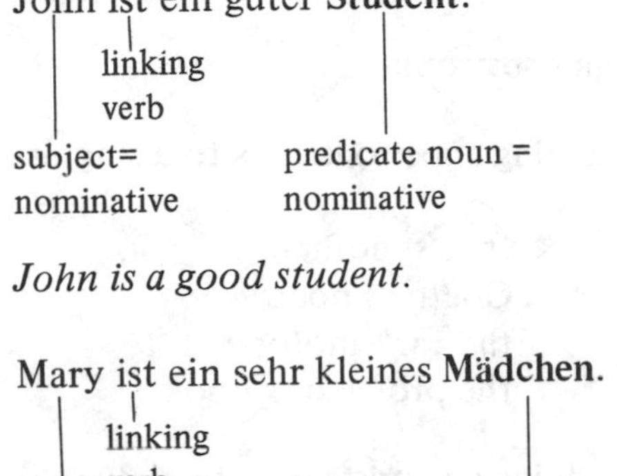

John is a good student.

Mary ist ein sehr kleines **Mädchen**.

linking verb

subject = nominative

predicate noun = nominative

Mary is a very small girl.

You should learn to recognize linking verbs like **sein** (*to be*), **werden** (*to become*), and **scheinen** (*to appear*), which often have a predicate noun with them.

<< What is the Possessive? >>

The term **possessive** means that one noun *possesses* or owns another noun.

In English: You can show possession in one of two ways:

1. With an **apostrophe**

   - by adding **apostrophe + s** to a singular possessor

     Inge*'s* mother
Goethe*'s* poetry
the car*'s* motor
the professor*'s* book

   - by adding an **apostrophe** to a plural possessor

     the girl*s'* father
the boy*s'* school

2. With the word ***of***

   - by adding ***of*** before a singular proper name

     the poetry *of* Goethe
the mother *of* Inge

   - by adding ***of the*** before other noun possessors

     the school *of the* boys
the coat *of the* woman
the father *of the* girls
the motor *of the* car

In German: There are also two ways of showing possession:

1. By using the genitive case. The genitive case is formed as follows:

- by adding -s to most proper names

  Inges Mutter
  Inge's mother

  Goethes Dichtung
  Goethe's poetry

  With proper names, the possessor comes before the thing possessed, just as in English.

- by adding -es to most masculine and neuter singular nouns of one syllable and -s to masculine and neuter nouns of more than one syllable. The accompanying articles likewise end in -s:

  der Motor des Autos
  the car's motor

  das Buch des Professors
  the professor's book

- by using the genitive ending -er on articles or adjectives preceding feminine and plural nouns. These nouns have no special genitive ending themselves.

  der Mantel d**er Frau**
  feminine singular

  The woman's coat

  der Vater d**er Mädchen**
  neuter plural

  the girls' father

  Kisten al**ter Bücher**
  neuter plural

  boxes of old books.

  As you can see, with nouns that are not proper nouns, the possessor follows the thing possessed.

Your German textbook will explain the genitive in further detail and will point out a few irregularities which occur with it.

2. By using *von* + **the dative case**. This structure corresponds to the English use of ***of*** to express possession.

   die Mutter **von** Inge
   *the mother **of** Inge*

   die Dichtung **von** Goethe
   *the poetry **of** Goethe*

   der Motor **vom** Auto
   von + dem = vom
   *the motor **of the** car*

   der Vater **von den** Mädchen
   *the father **of the** girls*

   In general, *von* + **the dative** is used to express possession in colloquial German while the genitive case is used in writing and in formal language.

<< What is a Pronoun? >>

A **pronoun** is a word used in place of one or more nouns. It may stand, therefore, for a person, place, thing, or idea.

For instance, instead of repeating the proper noun "Paul" in the following two sentences, we would use a pronoun in the second sentence:

Paul likes to sing. *Paul* goes to practice every day.
Paul likes to sing. *He* goes to practice every day.

A pronoun can only be used to refer to something (or someone) that has already been mentioned. The word that the pronoun replaces is called the **antecedent** of the pronoun.

In the example above, the pronoun *he* refers to the proper noun *Paul*. *Paul* is the antecedent of the pronoun *he*.

In English: There are different types of pronouns. They will be discussed in separate sections of this handbook. Below we will simply list the most important categories and refer you to the section where they are explained in detail.

Pronouns change in form in the different persons and according to the function they have in the sentence.

- **Personal Pronouns**–These pronouns change form in the different persons (1st, 2nd, or 3rd) (see p. 33).

  Subject pronouns–Personal pronouns used as the subject of a verb (see p. 33)

  I go. *They* read. *He* runs.

- **Object pronouns**–Personal pronouns used as

  - direct object (see p. 38)

    Paul loves *her*.
    Jane saw *them* at the theater.

  - indirect object (see p. 38)

    The boy wrote *me* the letter.
    John gave *us* the book.

  - object of preposition (see p. 38)

    Robert is going to the movies with *us*.
    Don't step on *it*; walk around *it*.

- **Reflexive Pronouns**–These pronouns refer back to the subject of the sentence (see p. 91).

    I cut *myself.*
    He spoke about *himself.*

- **Interrogative pronouns**–These pronouns are used in questions (see p. 97).

    Who is that?
    What do you want?

- **Possessive pronouns**–These pronouns are used to show possession (see p. 90).

    Whose book is that? *Mine. Yours* is on the table.

- **Relative pronouns**–These pronouns are used to introduce relative subordinate clauses (see p. 105).

    The man *who* came is very nice.
    Mary, *whom* you met, is president of the company.

In German: Pronouns are identified in the same way as in English. The most important difference is that German pronouns use more case forms than English pronouns do (see **What is Meant by Case?**, p. 11). Moreover, German pronouns agree with the nouns they replace; that is, they must correspond in gender and in number with their antecedents. You will find additional information in the individual sections on pronouns which follow.

<< What is a Personal Pronoun? >>

Both in English and in German the **personal pronouns** are those pronouns which have different forms for the different persons to which they refer:

I and *we*	used by the person(s) speaking; called 1st person pronouns
you	used for the person(s) spoken to; called 2nd person pronouns
he, *she*, *it*, *they*	used for the person(s) or thing(s) spoken about; called 3rd person pronouns

Some personal pronouns also show number; that is, they show whether one person or more than one is involved. *We* and *they* are plural pronouns; *I* and *he* are singular.

In both German and English, personal pronouns have different forms to show the pronouns' function in the sentence; these forms are called **case forms** (see **What is Meant by Case?**, p. 11). *We* and *us* are different cases of the first person plural pronoun, for example. The two most common functions of personal pronouns are as subject and object. These functions are discussed below.

A. <u>Personal pronouns as subjects</u>

In the following examples a personal pronoun is used as the subject:

> *He* ran, but *I* walked.
>
> Who ran? Answer: He.
> *He* is the subject of the verb *ran*.
>
> Who walked? Answer: I.
> *I* is the subject of the verb *walked*.

Let us compare the subject pronouns of English and German. In both languages, the form of the pronoun used for the subject is called the **nominative form** (see **What is Meant by Case?**, p. 11). Although the case system is much more developed in German than in English, understanding cases of pronouns in English can help you understand how cases work in German.

English nominative case		German nominative case
I	1st person singular the person speaking	**ich**
you	2nd person singular the person spoken to	**du/Sie**
he *she* *it*	3rd person singular the person or thing spoken about	**er** **sie** **er/sie/es**
we	1st person plural the person speaking + others *Mary and I* speak German. *we*	**wir**
you	2nd person plural the persons being spoken to	**ihr/Sie**
they	3rd person plural the persons or objects spoken about	**sie**

Let us look more closely at the two subject pronouns which have more than one German form so that you can learn how to choose the correct one.

You—the familiar and formal form

In English: There is no difference between "you" when it is being used to speak to a pet and when it is being used to speak to the President of the United States:

What are *you* chewing on, *you* silly dog?

Mr. President, what do *you* intend to do about energy conservation?

Likewise, there is no difference between "you" in the singular and "you" in the plural. For example, if there were many people in a room and you asked out loud, "Are *you* coming with me?," the "you" could stand for one person or for many.

In German: There is a difference between "you" in the singular and "you" in the plural; there is also a difference between the "you" used with close friends, the **familiar** *you*, and the "you" used with persons you do not know well, the **formal** *you*.

- **Familiar** *you*

The familiar forms of *you* are used with members of one's family, friends, children, and pets. In general, you use the familiar forms with persons you call by a first name.

du familiar singular *you*.
It can address one person.

Hans, was machst **du**?
*Hans, what are **you** doing?*

Inge, bist **du** jetzt endlich fertig?
*Inge, are **you** finished now?*

ihr familiar plural *you.*
It can address more than one person to whom you say **du.**

Maria und Inge, was macht **ihr**?
*Maria and Inge, what are **you** doing?*

Hans und Peter, kommt **ihr** mit?
*Hans and Peter, are **you** coming along?*

- **Formal** *you*

The formal form of *you* is used to address one or more persons you do not know very well. It is the same form (**Sie**) in both the singular and the plural, that is, if you are addressing one or more persons.

Herr Braun, kommen **Sie** mit?
*Mr. Braun, are **you** coming along?*

Herr und Frau Braun, kommen **Sie** mit?
*Mr. and Mrs. Braun, are **you** coming along?*

NOTE: When in doubt as to whether you should use the familiar or the formal form of you, use the formal form, unless you are speaking to a child or an animal.

It–the gender of the third person pronoun

In English: The neuter pronoun *it* is used to replace the noun for any object or idea.

Where is the book? *It* is on the table.
Where is the pencil? *It* is lying on the table.
Do you love freedom? *It* is precious.

In German: Since German nouns have a gender (see **What is Meant by Gender?**, p. 8), the pronouns which replace them must show the proper gender. Thus a pronoun will be either neuter, masculine, or feminine.

To choose the correct form of *it*, you must:

1. Find the noun *it* replaces (the antecedent).
2. Determine the gender of the antecedent in German.
3. Determine the function of *it* in the sentence.[1]
4. Choose the case which corresponds to the function found under step 3.

Below you will find an example of each gender:

- *Where is the book? **It** is on the table.*

  Noun *it* replaces: the book
  Gender: **Das Buch** is neuter.
  Function: subject of *is*
  Case: nominative

  Wo ist das Buch? **Es** ist auf dem Tisch.
  neuter singular
  subject pronoun = nominative

- *Where is the pencil? **It** is lying on the table.*

  Noun *it* replaces: the pencil
  Gender: **Der Bleistift** is masculine.
  Function: subject of *is lying*
  Case: nominative

  Wo ist der Bleistift? **Er** liegt auf dem Tisch.
  masculine singular
  subject pronoun = nominative

---

[1] Since this section is devoted to subject pronouns, *it* in all the examples below is a subject. Do not forget that *it* can also be an object. (See p. 40.)

- *Do you love freedom?* ***It*** *is precious.*

  Noun *it* replaces: freedom
  Gender: **Die Freiheit** is feminine.
  Function: subject of *is*
  Case: nominative

  Lieben Sie die Freiheit? **Sie** ist schön.

  feminine singular
  subject pronoun = nominative

B. Personal pronouns as objects

In the following examples a personal pronoun is used as an object.

He saw *us*.

He saw *whom*? Us.
Us is the direct object of *saw*.

They wrote *me*.

They wrote *to whom*? Me.
Me is the indirect object of *wrote*.

In English: The pronouns that occur as objects in a sentence are different from the ones used as subjects. When pronouns are used as the direct or indirect object or as the object of a preposition in English they are said to be in the **objective case** (see **What are Objects?**, p. 20).

He and *I* work for the newspaper.
subject = personal pronouns in *nominative* case

They invited *him* and *me*.
direct object = personal pronouns in *objective* case

I lent *them* my car.
indirect object = personal pronoun in *objective* case

They are coming with *you* and *her*.
object of a preposition = personal pronouns in *objective* case

Compare the nominative and objective cases of English pronouns:

Nominative	Objective
I	me
you	you
he	him
she	her
it	it
we	us
you	you
they	them

In German: Instead of a single objective case, there are two cases of pronouns which are used for pronoun objects: the accusative and the dative. (A third case, the genitive, occurs only rarely in personal pronouns.) The use of these different cases corresponds to the use of the same cases of nouns (see **What is Meant by Case?**, p. 11). The accusative and dative forms of the personal pronouns corresponding to the English ones above are as follows:

Nominative	Accusative	Dative
ich	mich	mir
du	dich	dir
er	ihn	ihm
sie	sie	ihr
es	es	ihm
wir	uns	uns
ihr	euch	euch
sie (*they*)	sie	ihnen
Sie (*you*)	Sie	Ihnen

In general, once you have learned the functions of German cases of nouns, you will have no difficulty using the cases of pronouns.

NOTE: Remember that German personal pronouns in the third person replace nouns having certain genders. (This has been discussed in detail for the third person in the nominative case on p. 37.) Make sure that the gender of the pronoun is the same as the gender of the noun that you are replacing.

- *Did you see the film?* Hast du **den Film** gesehen? (masculine singular)
  *Yes, I saw **it**.* Ja, ich habe **ihn** gesehen. (masculine singular accusative object)

- *Are you reading the newspaper?* Lesen Sie **die Zeitung**? (feminine singular)
  *Yes, I am reading **it**.* Ja, ich lese **sie**. (feminine singular accusative object)

- *Do you understand the book?* Verstehen Sie **das Buch**? (neuter singular)
  *Yes, I understand **it**.* Ja, ich verstehe **es**. (neuter singular accusative object)

There is a difference between English and German, however, when you replace a noun object of a preposition with a pronoun object of a preposition.

In English: We can replace any noun object of a preposition with a pronoun object. It can replace a person and a thing.

- a person

  John talked about *his sister*. (noun object of preposition) John talked about *her*. (pronoun object of preposition)

- a thing

  John talked about *his work*. (noun object of preposition) John talked about *it*. (pronoun object of preposition)

In German: We can replace the noun object of a preposition with a pronoun object only if the noun refers to a person. A different construction is used when the noun refers to a thing.

- a person

*John talked about **his sister**.*
John sprach von **seiner Schwester**.

preposition — von
noun object of preposition — seiner Schwester
feminine singular
von takes dative

*John talked about **her**.*
John sprach von **ihr**.

pronoun object of preposition — ihr
feminine singular to replace **Schwester**
von takes dative

- a thing

A pronoun, however, cannot be the object of a preposition if it refers to something other than a person. You will need to use a special construction, called a *da-* **compound** or a **pronominal adverb** (it is an adverb which takes the place of a preposition + a pronoun), every time you encounter the English construction **preposition** + *it*. It is formed by adding the prefix **da-** to the preposition.

*John talked about **his work**.*
John sprach von **seiner Arbeit**.

preposition — von
noun object of preposition — seiner Arbeit
(not a person)

*John talked **about it**.*
John sprach **davon.**

*Don't think **about it**.*
Denken Sie nicht **daran.**

Don't worry ***about it.***
Mach dir keine Sorgen **darum.**

I can't do anything ***about it.***
Ich kann nichts **dafür.**

Your German textbook will discuss this construction and its use in greater detail.

Summary: In deciding which form of a personal pronoun to use in a German sentence, you will need to ask yourself the following questions:

1. To which person does the pronoun refer?
   (1st, 2nd or 3rd - singular or plural)

   - If it is the 2nd person, keep in mind the distinction between the familiar and formal *you*.

   - If it is the 3rd person singular, remember to have the gender of the pronoun agree with the gender of the noun replaced.

2. How does the pronoun function in the sentence?
   (subject, direct object, indirect object, etc.)

   They live in Vienna.
   subject

   We know *him.*
   direct object

   We wrote *her* a letter.
   indirect object

   They talked about *us.*
   personal object of preposition

   They talked about *it.*
   non-personal object of preposition

3. What case in German is required for that particular function of the pronoun?

They live in Vienna.
subject=nominative

We know *him*.
direct object=accusative

We wrote *her* a letter.
indirect object=dative

They talked about *us*.
personal object of preposition
about=**von**
von requires a dative object

They talked about *it*.
non-personal object of preposition
requires a **da**-compound
about it=**da+von**

4. Select the proper form (gender, number and case) according to steps 1-3.

***They** live in Vienna.*
Sie wohnen in Wien.
3rd person plural nominative

We know ***him.***
Wir kennen **ihn.**
3rd person masculine singular accusative

We wrote ***her*** *a letter.*
Wir haben **ihr** einen Brief geschrieben.
3rd person feminine singular dative

*They talked about **us**.*
Sie haben von **uns** gesprochen

1st person plural dative with **von**

*They talked about **it**.*
Sie haben **davon** gesprochen.

da-compound
replacing **von** + impersonal object

< < What is a Verb? > >

A **verb** is a word that expresses an action, mental state, or condition. The action can be physical, as in such verbs as *run*, *walk*, *hit*, *sit*, or mental, as in such verbs as *dream*, *think*, *believe*, and *hope*. Verbs like *be* and *become* express a state or condition rather than an action.

The verb is one of the most important words of a sentence; you cannot express a complete thought (i.e., write a **complete sentence**) without a verb.

To help you learn to recognize verbs, here is a paragraph where the verbs are in italics:

> The three students ***entered*** the restaurant, ***selected*** a table, ***hung*** up their coats and ***sat*** down. They ***looked*** at the menu and ***asked*** the waitress what she ***recommended***. She ***advised*** the daily special, beef stew. It ***was*** not expensive. They ***chose*** a bottle of red wine and ***ordered*** a salad. The service ***was*** slow, but the food ***tasted*** excellent. Good cooking, they ***decided***, ***takes*** time. They ***ordered*** pastry for dessert and ***finished*** the meal with coffee.

A **transitive verb** is a verb which takes a direct object. (See **What are Objects?**, p. 20.) It is indicated by a (*v.t.*) in the dictionary.

The boy *threew* the ball. (ball: direct object)	to throw–transitive verb
She *lost* her job. (job: direct object)	to lose–transitive verb

An **intransitive verb** is a verb that does not take a direct object. It is indicated by (*v.i.*) in the dictionary.

Paul *is sleeping.*	to sleep–intransitive verb
She *arrives* today. (today: adverb)	to arrive–intransitive verb

Many verbs can be used both transitively and intransitively, depending on whether or not they have a direct object in the sentence.

The students *speak* German. (German: direct object)	to speak–transitive verb
Actions *speak* louder than words. (louder: adverb)	to speak–intransitive verb

<< What are the Principal Parts of a Verb? >>

The **principal parts** of a verb are those forms which we need to know in order to form all the different tenses.

In English: If we know **the infinitive**, **the past tense**, and the **past participle** of any verb, we can apply regular rules to form all the other tenses of that verb. These three forms constitute the principal parts of an English verb.

For example, in order to form the six main tenses of the verb ***to eat***, we need to know the parts *eat* (the form used in the infinitive), *ate* (simple past), and *eaten* (past participle):

Present	I eat
Present Perfect	I have eaten
Past	I ate
Past Perfect	I had eaten
Future	I shall eat
Future Perfect	I shall have eaten

The principal parts of a verb are either regular or irregular:

- **Regular verbs** form their past tense and their past participle very predictably by simply adding *-ed*, *-d*, **or** *-t* **to the base of the infinitive**:

Infinitive	Past Tense	Past Participle
to walk	walked	walked
to seem	seemed	seemed
to burn	burned or burnt	burned or burnt

Since the past tense and the past participle of regular verbs are identical, these verbs really have only two principal parts, the infinitive and the simple past form.

- **Irregular verbs** have unpredictable principal parts. As we grow up, we learn these forms simply by hearing them, although some of them give us difficulty and require extra effort to master. Examples of verbs with irregular principal parts include the following:

Infinitive	Past Tense	Past Participle
to sing	sang	sung
to draw	drew	drawn
to hit	hit	hit
to lie	lay	lain
to ride	rode	ridden

In German: The principal parts are basically the same as in English: the infinitive, the past tense, and the past participle. Some verbs have a fourth principal part, which is discussed below.

German verbs fall into two categories on the basis of their formation of principal parts:

1. weak verbs
2. strong verbs

1. **Weak verbs** resemble English regular verbs in that they form their principal parts predictably:

- They form their past tense by adding a **-t-** (or if the verb stem ends in **-d** or **-t**, an **-et-**) to the stem of the infinitive and then adding a set of endings for each person.

- They form their past participle by adding the prefix **ge-** and the suffix **-t** or **-et** to the stem of the verb.

Infinitive	Past Tense (1st per. sing.)	Past Participle
machen	mach**te**	**ge**mach**t**
arbeiten	arbeit**ete**	**ge**arbeit**et**
glauben	glaub**te**	**ge**glaub**t**

2. **Strong verbs** have unpredictable principle parts. You simply will have to memorize them as new vocabulary.

- The vowel of the infinitive stem may change in the past and in the past participle.
- The past participle always ends in **-en**. There is no additional **-t** in either the past tense or the past participle as there is in the weak verbs.

Infinitive	Past Tense (1st per. sing.)	Past Participle
finden	fand	(hat)[1] gefunden
kommen	kam	(ist) gekommen
verlieren	verlor	(hat) verloren
singen	sang	(hat) gesungen

- Some strong verbs also have a change of the stem vowel in the 2nd and 3rd person singular of the present tense, introducing a fourth principal part for you to learn:

Infinitive	Past Tense	Past Participle	3rd per. sing. pres.
laufen	lief	(ist) gelaufen	läuft
lesen	las	(hat) gelesen	liest
schlafen	schlief	(hat) geschlafen	schläft
nehmen	nahm	(hat) genommen	er nimmt

Only by learning the principal parts of these verbs can you conjugate them properly in all their tenses.

[1] Because the past participle is used as part of the perfect tense, it is wise to memorize the proper auxiliary verb when you memorize the principal parts.

< < What is an Infinitive? > >

An **infinitive** is a form of the verb. It is the form of the verb found in the dictionary as the main entry. The infinitive can never be used as the main verb of a sentence; there must always be another verb with it, a verb that is conjugated. A verb in its conjugated form is often called a finite verb to contrast it with an infinitive.

In English: The infinitive is composed of two words, ***to* + verb**: *to be*, *to walk*, *to think*, *to enjoy*. The infinitive is always used with a conjugated verb. (See **What is a Verb Conjugation?**, p. 50.)

To learn *is* challenging.
infinitive — main verb

It *is* important ***to be*** on time.
main verb — infinitive

Bob and Mary *want* ***to play*** tennis.
main verb — infinitive

It *has started* ***to rain***.
main verb — infinitive

In German: The infinitive is composed of only one word, which ends with the letters **-n** or **-en**. It is used in a variety of ways; it can never serve as the main or only verb in a sentence. There will always be another conjugated verb with it.

*Bob wants **to play** tennis.*
Bob will Tennis **spielen**.
conjugated verb — infinitive

<< What is a Verb Conjugation? >>

A **verb conjugation** is a list of the six possible forms of the verb, one form for each of the subject pronouns. Conjugations are always learned with pronouns.

In English: Verbs change very little. Let us look at the various forms the verb ***to sing*** takes in English in the present tense when each of the six possible pronouns is the performer of the action.

1st per. sing.	***I sing*** with the music.
2nd per. sing.	***You sing*** with the music.
3rd per. sing.	***He sings*** with the music. ***She sings*** with the music. ***It sings*** with the music.
1st per. pl.	***We sing*** with the music.
2nd per. pl.	***You sing*** with the music.
3rd per. pl.	***They sing*** with the music.

English verb conjugation is very simple. Most verbs, like ***to sing***, have only two forms: *sing* and *sings*. The verb ***to be*** has the most forms: I *am*, you *are*, he *is*.

In German: German verbs have many more forms than English verbs. Most verbs have four different forms. Fortunately, the formation of these forms is quite predictable in most verbs, once you have learned a few simple rules.

A. Let us look at the same verb ***to sing*** that we conjugated in English, paying special attention now to the personal subject pronoun (see p. 33):

1st per. sing.	**ich** singe
2nd per. familiar sing.	**du** singst
3rd per. sing.	**er** singt **sie** singt **es** singt

1st per. pl.	**wir** singen
2nd per. familiar pl.	**ihr** singt
3rd per. pl.	**sie** singen
2nd per. formal sing. & pl.	**Sie** singen

You will have few problems knowing when to use the three singular persons (*I*, *you*, *he/she/it*–**ich**, **du**, **er/sie/es**), but you may confuse the three plural persons. Let us go over them.

- **1st person plural**–The *we form* of the verb is used whenever *I* (the speaker) is one of the doers of the action; that is, whenever the speaker is included in a plural or multiple subject:

The students and I *sing* when the term is over.
In German: **wir** form

Paul, Peter, Mary and I *sing* all day long.
In German: **wir** form

In the two sentences above, the subject could be replaced by the pronoun *we*; thus in German you must use the **wir** form (1st person plural of the verb).

- **2nd person plural familiar**–The *you plural familiar form* of the verb is used whenever you are addressing more than one person to whom you say **du**.

Peter, *are* you *coming* along?
In German: **du** form

Peter and Mary, *are* you finished yet?
In German: **ihr** form

- **3rd person plural**—The *they form* of the verb is used whenever you are speaking about a plural or multiple subject which does not include either the speaker or the person being spoken to:

  The boys *sing* when the term is over.
  In German: **sie** form

  Paul, Peter, and Henry *sing* all day long.
  In German: **sie** form

  (Compare with Paul, Peter, Henry, and I *sing* . . . .)
  In German: **wir** form

  The glasses and the cokes *are* on the counter.
  In German: **sie** form

  In the three sentences above, the subject could be replaced by the pronoun *they*; thus in German you must use the **sie** form, the 3rd person plural of the verb.

- **2nd person formal, singular and plural**—The *formal you form* of the verb, singular and plural, is used whenever you are addressing one or more persons to whom you say **Sie**:

  Mrs. Smith, *are* you *coming* along with us?
  In German: **Sie** form

  Mr. and Mrs. Smith, *are* you *coming* along with us?
  In German: **Sie** form

B. Let us now look at the same verb ***to sing***, paying special attention to the verb form.

ich sing**e**

du sing**st**

er sing**t**
sie sing**t**
es sing**t**

wir sing**en**

ihr sing**t**

sie sing**en**

Sie sing**en**

We speak of there being two parts to a German verb:

1. **the stem**, which we obtain by dropping the final **-en** from the infinitive (or with a few verbs like **tun** and **ändern** by dropping the final **-n**).

Infinitive	Stem
sing**en**	sing-
mach**en**	mach-
komm**en**	komm-

2. **the personal endings**, which change for each person, with some overlapping.

   As you can see in the verb **singen** conjugated above, the endings for the present tense are **-e**, **-st**, **-t**, **-en**, **-t**, **-en**.

Some verb stems require slight adjustments in the endings. Your German textbook will explain the rules for these adjustments. A very few German verbs are irregular in the present tense, that is, they do not follow any regular pattern and must be memorized individually. In addition, some of the so-called strong verbs (see **What is a Participle?**, p. 62) have a stem change in the **du-** and **er/sie/es** form of the present tense. Again, you must simply memorize these verbs.

<< What is Meant by Tense? >>

The **tense** of a verb indicates the time when the action of the verb takes place: at the **present** time, in the **past**, or in the **future**, for example.

I *am eating.*	Present
I *ate.*	Past
I *shall eat.*	Future

As you can see in the above examples, just by putting the verb in a different tense and without giving any additional information (such as "I am eating *now*," "I ate *yesterday*," "I shall eat *tomorrow*"), you can indicate when the action of the verb takes place. There are six main tenses in English: present, present perfect, past, past perfect, future, and future perfect. This handbook discusses each of these tenses in separate sections.

<< What is the Present Tense? >>

The **present tense** indicates that the action is going on at the present time. It can be:

- at the time the speaker is speaking

  I *see* you.

- a habitual action

  He *smokes* when he *is* nervous.

- a general truth

  The sun *shines* every day.

In English: There are three forms of the verb which, although they have a slightly different meaning, all indicate the present tense.

Mary *studies* in the library.	Present
Mary *is studying* in the library.	Present progressive
Mary *does study* in the library.	Present emphatic

In German: There is only one verb form to indicate the present tense. It is indicated by the ending of the verb, without any helping verb such as *is* and *does*. It is very important, therefore, not to translate these helping verbs used in English. Simply put the main verb in the present.

Mary *studies* at the university.
studiert

Mary *is studying* at the university.
studiert

Mary *does study* at the university.
studiert

<< What is the Past Tense? >>

The **past tense** is used to express an action that occurred in the past.

In English: There are several verb forms that indicate that the action took place in the past.

I worked	Simple past
I was working	Past progressive
I did work	Past emphatic

The simple past is called "simple" because it consists of only one word. The past progressive and the past emphatic are called "compound" tenses because they consist of more than one word.

English also has three other compound tenses for expressing past actions. These are the **perfect tenses**.

I have worked	Present perfect
I had worked	Past perfect
I shall have worked	Future perfect

These last three tenses will be discussed in a separate section (see **What are the Perfect Tenses?**, p. 69).

In German: There is no way of expressing the difference of meaning between the English simple past (*I worked*), the past progressive (*I was working*), and the past emphatic (*I did work*).[1] German does have two tenses for expressing an action which occurred in the past.

These two tenses cannot, however, be matched up with the English tenses.

---

[1] Notice the similarity with the English and German present tense. See. p. 55.

The two German tenses for expressing action in the past are the simple past and the perfect.

1. The **simple past** consists of only one word. This tense is also called the **imperfect (Imperfekt)** or the **preterite (Präteritum)**.

2. The German **perfect** tense **(Perfekt)** is a compound tense, consisting of two parts.

The formation of both the simple past and the perfect depends on whether the verb is a so-called strong verb or a weak verb. (See **What are the Principal Parts of a Verb?**, p. 46.) Your German textbook will explain in detail the rules for the formation of these two tenses for both groups of verbs.

It is important to remember that these two tenses do not express a difference in meaning; instead, their difference is one of style: the perfect is used for a conversational style, and the simple past is used for a narrative style.

Do not let yourself be fooled by the fact that the German perfect tense has the same basic structure as the English present perfect: both are formed by an auxiliary verb in the present tense (in German either **haben** or **sein**; in English *to have*) + the past participle.

Look at the structural similarity of these two tenses:

ich	habe	gesehen
subject	auxiliary verb	past participle
I	*have*	*seen*

Ilse	hat	gegessen
subject	auxiliary verb	past participle
Ilse	*has*	*eaten*

Don't be confused by this structural similarity. **Ich habe gesehen** is usually not best translated as *I have seen*, nor is **Ilse hat**

gegessen best translated as *Ilse has eaten*. It is best to think of both the German simple past and the German perfect as equivalent to the English simple past:

Perfect	ich habe gesehen	Simple past	*I saw*
Simple past	ich sah		
Perfect	Ilse hat gegessen	Simple past	*Ilse ate*
Simple past	Ilse aß		

For further discussion of the English present perfect tense and its equivalents in German, see **What are the Perfect Tenses?**, p. 69.

< < What are Auxiliary Verbs? > >

Verbs that work together with another verb are called **auxiliary verbs** or **helping verbs**.

Mary *is* a girl.	*is*	main verb
Paul *has* a headache.	*has*	main verb
They *go* to the movies.	*go*	main verb
They ***have*** *gone* to the movies. (complete verb)	***have***	auxiliary verb
	gone	main verb
She ***has been*** *gone* for three hours. (complete verb)	***has***	auxiliary verb
	been	auxiliary verb
	gone	main verb

In English: The three main auxiliary verbs are ***to have***, ***to be***, and ***to do***. They have three main uses:

1. to help formulate questions

Bob *has* a dog.	*has*	main verb
Does Bob *have* a dog?	***does***	auxiliary verb
complete verb	*have*	main verb

2. to show the tense of the complete verb in the sentence (present, future, past—see **What is Meant by Tense?**, p. 54)

Mary ***is** reading* a book.	Present
Mary ***will** read* a book.	Future
Mary ***was** reading* a book.	Past

3. to indicate the passive voice (see **What is Meant by Active and Passive Voice?**, p. 142)

The book ***is** read* by many people.

English also has a group of auxiliary verbs called **modal auxiliaries**. These verbs, for example ***can***, ***may***, ***should***, ***must***, show that the action expressed by the other verb in the sentence is not occurring:

John ***can** read* this book.
John ***may** read* this book.
John ***must** read* this book.
John ***should** read* this book.

In German: The three main auxiliary verbs are **haben** (*to have*), **sein** (*to be*), and **werden** (*to become*).

1. **Haben** and **sein** are used as auxiliaries to form the perfect tenses of verbs; some verbs use **haben** and some use **sein**. (See **What are the Perfect Tenses?**, p. 69.)

- Der Mann **hat** seine Zeitung **gefunden.**

  auxiliary verb — past participle of **finden**

  hat gefunden (present perfect)

  *The man **has found** his newspaper.*

- Der Student **war** sehr spät **gekommen.**

  auxiliary verb — past participle of **kommen**

  war gekommen (pluperfect)

  *The student **had come** very late.*

2. **Werden** is used to form the future tenses and the passive voice. (See **What is the Future Tense?**, p. 73, and **What is Meant by Active and Passive Voice?**, p. 142.)

- Sie **werden zahlen.**

  auxiliary verb — infinitive

  werden zahlen (future tense)

  *They **will pay**.*

- Das Haus **wird** jetzt **gebaut.**

  auxiliary verb — past participle of **bauen**

  wird gebaut (passive voice, present tense)

  *The house **is** now **being built**.*

German also has a group of auxiliary verbs called modal auxiliaries: **können** (*to be able*), **sollen** (*to be supposed to*), **müssen** (*to be obligated to*), **wollen** (*to want to*), **dürfen** (*to be permitted to*), and **mögen** (*to like to*). These are usually used with the infinitive of another verb.

- Inge **will mitkommen.**

  modal auxiliary — infinitive
  present tense

  *Inge **wants to come** along.*

- Der Zug **sollte** pünktlich **ankommen.**

  modal auxiliary — infinitive
  past tense

  *The train **was supposed to arrive** on time.*

You will find that German and English often do not overlap in their use of auxiliaries.

1. The English auxiliary verbs *do, does, did* do not exist as separate auxiliary verbs in German. When you encounter them in an English sentence which you are trying to express in German, you should use them as a guideline for tense, but you must not translate them.

   ***Does** John **live** here?*
   ignore — German verb present tense

   Wohnt John hier?
   lives John here

2. English often uses a form of the verb *to be* as an auxiliary verb with a present participle. (See **What is a Participle?**, p. 62.)

   *We **are working** today.*
   auxiliary verb — present participle

German does not use this construction. Here again you should ignore the verb *are* and concentrate on the German equivalent of *work* in the present tense. (See **What is the Present Tense?**, p. 55.)

Wir **arbeiten** heute.
we work today

< < What is a Participle? > >

A **participle** has two functions: 1. It is a form of the verb that is used in combination with an auxiliary verb to indicate certain tenses. 2. It may be used as an adjective or modifier to describe something.

I *was writing* a letter.
auxiliary participle

The *broken* vase was on the floor.
participle describing *vase*

There are two types of participles: the **present participle** and the **past participle**. As you will learn in your study of German, participles are not used in the same way in the two languages.

A. The **present participle**

In English: The present participle is easy to recognize because it is an ***-ing*** form of the verb: work*ing*, study*ing*, danc*ing*, play*ing*, etc.

The present participle is used:

- as part of the complete verb

She is *singing*.
They were *dancing*.

- as an attributive adjective (see p. 116)

This is an *amazing* discovery.
describes the noun *discovery*

She read an *interesting* book.
describes the noun *book*

- as an adjective in a participial phrase (see p. 153)

  Turning the corner, Tony ran into a tree.

  The entire phrase *turning the corner* works as an adjective describing *Tony*.

  Look at the cat *climbing the tree*.

  Climbing the tree works as an adjective describing *cat*.

In German: The present participle is formed by adding **-d** to the infinitive.

Infinitive	Present participle
singen	singend
spielen	spielend
sprechen	sprechend
schweigen	schweigend

German, like English, uses the present participle as an adjective but primarily as an attributive adjective.

die **singenden** Kinder	*the **singing** children*
ein **spielendes** Mädchen	*a **playing** girl*
die laut **sprechende** Frau	*the loudly **talking** woman*

In such usage, the participle functions like any other attributive adjective, and its endings depend on three things:

1. Does an article precede it, and is the article definite (**der, die, das**) or indefinite (**ein, eine, ein**)?
2. What is the gender and number of the noun it modifies?
3. What is the case of the noun?

Look at **What is an Adjective?**, p. 115, for additional help and examples.

However, the present participle is not always used in the same way in German as in English.

As a beginner, you must keep in mind that the equivalents of common English tenses formed with an auxiliary + present participle (*she is singing*, *they are dancing*) do not use participles in German. These English constructions correspond to a German tense of the verb:

She ***is singing.***
Sie **singt.**
present

They ***were dancing.***
Sie **tanzten.**
simple past

He ***will be writing.***
Er **wird schreiben.**
future

Here are some pointers to help you avoid making mistakes in using the present participle:

1. In German the present participle is used less frequently than in English.

2. Never assume that an English word ending with *-ing* is translated by its German counterpart ending in **-d**. Consult your German textbook for rules regarding the use of the present participle.

An English verb ending in *-ing* is not always a present participle; it can be a verbal noun. A **verbal noun** is a form of a verb which functions as a noun in a sentence. It is also often called a **gerund**. Since verbal nouns are rendered differently in German from present participles, we will discuss them here so that you can learn to distinguish them.

In English: The verbal noun ends in ***-ing*** and can function in a sentence in almost any way that a noun can. It can be a subject, direct object, indirect object and an object of a preposition.

Reading can be fun.

noun from the verb *to read*
subject of the sentence

Do you enjoy *singing*?

noun from the verb *to sing*
direct object of the sentence

We have often thought about *moving* away.

noun from the verb *to move*
object of preposition *about*

In German: These verbal nouns are usually expressed by a neuter noun made from the infinitive of the verb.

lesen	*to read*	das Lesen	*reading*
singen	*to sing*	das Singen	*singing*

You can recognize these *-ing* words as verbal nouns if you look carefully at their function in the sentence as in the examples given above.

B. The **past participle**

In English: This is the form you would use following *I have*.

1. The "regular" verbs form their past participle by adding ***-ed***, ***-d***, or ***-t*** to the basic form of the verb.

Basic verb	Past Participle
help	help*ed*
walk	walk*ed*
burn	burn*ed* or burn*t*

2. The "irregular" verbs form their past participle by changing their stem vowel (see p. 46) or by making other changes. Many of the most common English verbs are irregular.

Basic verb	Past Participle
go	gone
ride	ridden
speak	spoken

Notice that often, though not always, the past participle of irregular English verbs ends in *-n*.

The past participle is used

- as an attributive adjective (see p. 116)

Is the *written* word more important than the *spoken* word?

Written describes the noun *word*.
Spoken describes the noun *word*.

- as a verb form in combination with the auxiliary verbs *have* or *be*

I *have written* all that I have to say.
He *hasn't spoken* to me since our quarrel.
Truer words *were* never *spoken*.
This book *was written* several years ago.

In German: As in English, there are two groups of verbs:

1. the **weak verbs**, which form their past participle according to a regular rule, and

2. the **strong verbs**, which have irregular past participles.

1. The past participles of **weak verbs** are formed by adding

   - **ge-** to the front of the stem. Because it is placed before the stem it is called a prefix (see **What are Prefixes and Suffixes?**, p. 136).
   - **-t** to the end of the stem. Because it is placed after the stem it is called a suffix.

Infinitive	Stem	Past Participle	
machen	mach-	gemacht	*made*
glauben	glaub-	geglaubt	*believed*

   Some verb stems require slight adjustments. There are special rules for forming the past participle of verbs which already begin with prefixes. Your German textbook will explain how to handle these verbs.

2. The past participles of **strong verbs** often change the vowel in the stem, and sometimes some of the consonants. However, they all

   - add the **ge-** prefix to the front of the stem (unless the infinitive already has a prefix)
   - end in **-en**

Infinitive	Past Participle	
schlafen	geschlafen	*slept*
gehen	gegangen	*gone*
finden	gefunden	*found*
liegen	gelegen	*lain*

   As you can tell from this list, there is no way of predicting the past participle of a strong verb in German. You simply have to memorize it as the verb is presented in the vocabulary of your German textbook. It is important to remember, however, that the past participle of strong verbs always ends in **-en**, while the past participle of weak verbs always ends in **-t**. As with weak verbs, there are special rules for forming the past participle of strong verbs which already begin with a prefix.

German, like English, uses the past participle as an adjective and as part of the verb:

- as an attributive adjective

  In such usage, the rules about endings are the same as for any other attributive adjective. Look at **What is an Adjective?**, p. 115 for a list of the steps to follow to choose the proper ending.

  Ich verstehe **die gesprochene Sprache** nicht.
  I do not understand ***the spoken language****.*

  Die eingeladenen Gäste sind alle gekommen.
  The invited guests *all came.*

- as a verb form

  The most important use of the past participle in German is as part of a verb combination: all the perfect tenses are formed with an auxiliary verb, either *haben* (*to have*) **or** *sein* (*to be*) **+ the past participle**. Look at **What are the Perfect Tenses?**, p. 69, for a detailed study of this use of the past participle.

  The passive voice is formed with the auxiliary verb *werden* (*to become*) **+ the past participle**. Look at **What is Meant by Active and Passive Voice?**, p. 142, for more information on this usage.

<< What are the Perfect Tenses? >>

The **perfect tenses** are compound tenses of the verb made up of the **auxiliary verb** *to have* **+ the past participle**.

I *have* not *seen* him.
auxiliary verb — *have*; past participle of *to see* — *seen*

They *had* already *gone*.
auxiliary verb — *had*; past participle of *to go* — *gone*

As you can see, the auxiliary verb *to have* can be put in different tenses: for example, *I have* is the present tense; *they had* is the past tense.

In English: There are three main perfect tenses formed with the auxiliary verb *to have* **+ the past participle of the main verb**. (See **What is a Participle?**, p. 62.)

The name of each perfect tense is based on the tense used for the auxiliary verb.

1. **present perfect**: *to have* in the *present* tense + the past participle of the main verb.

I *have* ***eaten.***
auxiliary verb — *have*; past participle of *to eat* — ***eaten***

The boys *have* ***washed*** the car.
auxiliary verb — *have*; past participle of *to wash* — ***washed***

2. **past perfect** (pluperfect): *to have* in the simple *past* tense + the past participle of the main verb.

I *had* ***eaten*** before 6:00.

auxiliary verb — past participle of *to eat*

The boys *had* ***washed*** the car before the storm.

auxiliary verb — past participle of *to wash*

3. **future perfect**: *to have* in the *future* tense + the past participle of the main verb.

I *shall have* ***eaten*** by 6:00.

auxiliary verb — past participle of *to eat*

The boys *will have* ***washed*** the car by Thursday.

auxiliary verb — past participle of *to wash*

In German: As in English there are three perfect tenses; they are the perfect **(Perfekt)**, the past perfect or pluperfect **(Plusquamperfekt)** and the future perfect, which occurs very infrequently. These are all formed by the auxiliary verb ***haben* or *sein* + the past participle**. You must memorize which verbs require **sein** and which require **haben** as the auxiliary in the perfect tense.

1. **perfect tense**: **haben** or **sein** in the *present* tense + past participle of the main verb.

Wir **sind** ins Kino **gegangen**.
*We **went** to the movies.*

Wir **haben** den Film **gesehen**.
*We **saw** the film.*

Although this tense is structurally similar to the English present perfect (see **What is the Past Tense?**, p. 56), it is not used the same as the English present perfect. Often it is best translated into English by a simple past:

Ich **habe gegessen**.	*I* ***ate***.	Simple past
	I ***have eaten***.	Present perfect

Sometimes an adverb of time can help you decide how to interpret a German verb in the perfect tense.

Gestern habe ich zuviel gegessen.
Yesterday *I ate too much.*
adverb of time simple past

(Awkward: "Yesterday I have eaten too much.")

Ich habe **schon** zuviel gegessen.
I have ***already*** *eaten too much.*
adverb of time present perfect

(Awkward: "I already ate too much.")

You will need to study your German textbook for more detailed explanations of the uses of the German perfect.

2. **past perfect** or **pluperfect**: **haben** or **sein** in the *simple past* tense + past participle of the main verb. This tense resembles the English past perfect both in structure and in use. It expresses an action completed in the past before some other past action or event.

Wir **waren** ins Kino **gegangen**.
simple past of **sein**

We ***had gone*** *to the movies.*

Wir **hatten** den Film **gesehen.**
simple past of **haben**

*We **had seen** the film.*

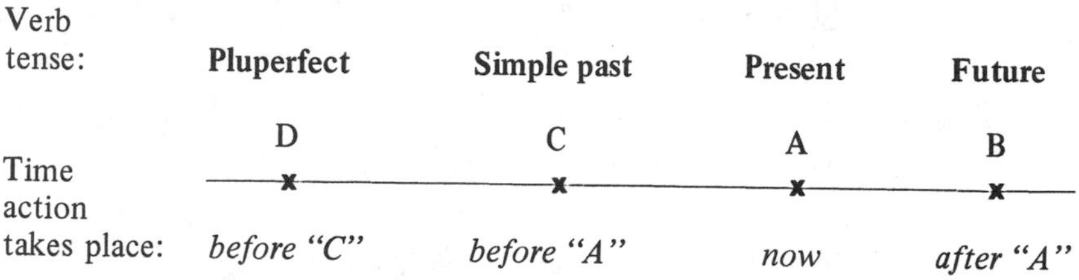

Verb tense:	**Pluperfect**	**Simple past**	**Present**	**Future**
	D	C	A	B
Time action takes place:	*before "C"*	*before "A"*	*now*	*after "A"*

*They **had** already **left** when I **arrived**.*

Sie **waren** schon **abgefahren** als ich **ankam.**
pluperfect "D". simple past "C"

*After we **had eaten**, we **took** a walk.*

Nachdem wir **gegessen hatten, machten** wir einen Spaziergang.
pluperfect "D" simple past "C"

3. **future perfect**: **haben** or **sein** in the *future* tense + past participle of the main verb.

Wir **werden** den Film **gesehen haben.**
future tense **haben**

*We **will have seen** the film.*

This tense is used like the English future perfect. It expresses an action which will be completed in the future before some other specific action or event occurs in the future.

Verb tense:	Present		Future Perfect		Future
	A		B		C
Time action takes place:	*now*		*after "A" and before "C"*		*after "A"*

They ***will have left*** *before I arrive.*

Sie **werden abgefahren sein**, bevor ich ankomme.

You should learn to recognize this tense.

< < What is the Future Tense? > >

The **future tense** is used to describe an action which will take place in the future.

In English: It is formed by means of the auxiliary verb *will* **or** *shall* **+ the main verb.**

Paul and Mary *will do* their homework tomorrow.
I *shall go* out tonight.

In German: The future tense is formed by the auxiliary verb *werden* (literally *to become*) **+ the infinitive of the main verb.** The conjugated verb **werden** agrees with the subject and the infinitive remains unchanged.

Paul and Mary ***will write*** *their homework.*

Paul und Mary **werden** ihre Hausaufgabe **schreiben.**

3rd per. pl. — infinitive

I ***shall go*** *out tonight.*

Ich **werde** heute abend **ausgehen.**

1st per. sing. — infinitive

Note the word order in the above German sentences: the infinitive stands at the end of the sentence.

The future tense in German is used much less frequently than in English. Often German will use the present tense with an adverb of future time instead of using the future tense of the verb. We do this in English too but less frequently.

- *Paul and Mary* ***are writing*** *their test* ***tomorrow.***

  present tense — adverb of future time

  Paul und Mary **schreiben morgen** ihre Prüfung.

- *I* ***am going*** *out soon.*

  present — adverb of future time

  Ich **gehe gleich** aus.

German also uses the future tense with the adverbs **wohl** (*probably*), **sicher** (*certainly*), **wahrscheinlich** (*probably*), and **vielleicht** (*perhaps*) to express probability. In such usage, the future tense has no future meaning–it refers simply to a probability in the present time. This is sometimes called the **future of probability**. You should not translate such sentences with a future tense in English.

Hans **wird** wohl schon zu Hause **sein**.

future tense

Hans ***is*** *probably at home now.*

Sie **werden** dieses Buch sicher **kennen**.

future tense

*You surely **know** this book.*

< < What is Meant by Mood? > >

The word mood is a variation of the word *mode*, meaning manner or way. The mood is the form of the verb which indicates the attitude (mode) of the speaker toward what he is saying. As a beginning student of German, all you have to know are the names of the moods so that you will understand what your German textbook is referring to. You will learn when to use the various moods as you learn verbs and their tenses.

In English: Verbs can be in one of three moods:

1. The **indicative mood** is used to express or indicate facts. This is the most common mood, and most verb forms that you use in everyday conversation belong to the indicative mood.

   Robert *studies* German.
   Mary *is* here.

   The present tense (see p. 55), the past tense (see p. 56), and the future tense (see p. 73) are all examples of tenses in the indicative mood.

2. The **imperative mood** is used to express a command. (See p. 76.)

   Robert, *study* German now!
   Mary, *be* here on time!

3. The **subjunctive mood** is used to express an action that is not really occurring. (See p. 78.)

   The professor insists that Robert *study* German.
   I wish that Mary *were* here.

In German: These same three moods exist and have their own special forms. Although the indicative is the most common mood, as it is in English, the subjunctive is also very important in German. (See **What is the Subjunctive?**, p. 78.)

< < What is the Imperative? > >

The **imperative** is the mood of the verb used for commands. It is used to give someone an order.

In English: There are two types of commands:

1. The *you* **command** is used when giving an order to one person or many persons. The dictionary form of the verb is used for the *you* command.

   Answer the phone.
   Clean your room.
   Talk softly.

Notice that the pronoun "you" is not stated. The absence of the pronoun *you* in the sentence is a good indication that you are dealing with an imperative and not a present tense. Compare the following sentences:

Present tense (statement)	→	Imperative (command)
You answer the phone	→	*Answer* the phone.
You clean your room.	→	*Clean* your room.
You talk softly.	→	*Talk* softly.

2. The *we* **command** is used when the speaker gives an order to himself as well as to others. In English this command begins with the phrase "let's" followed by the dictionary form of the verb.

   Let's leave.
   Let's go to the movies.

In German: The same two types of imperative exist. However, the *you* command has three different forms, according to the three different personal pronouns for *you*: **du, ihr** and **Sie** (see **What is a Personal Pronoun?**, p. 33). In all forms except the **du**- form, the verb is the same as the present tense indicative. In written German an exclamation point is used after an imperative.

- In the two familiar forms of the imperative, the subject pronoun is dropped, as in English:

du-form	**Höre**![1]	*Listen.*
	Schreibe mir bald!	*Write me soon.*
ihr-form	**Kommt** mit!	*Come along.*
	Eßt nicht so schnell, Kinder!	*Don't eat so fast, children.*

[1] The final **-e** on **höre** and **schreibe** is optional in conversational German.

- In the formal form, the subject pronoun is included and is placed directly after the **Sie**-form of the present tense.

Sie-form	**Sprechen Sie** lauter!	*Speak more loudly.*
	Kommen Sie mit!	*Come along.*

- In the *we*-form, the subject pronoun is included and is placed directly after the **wir**-form of the present tense.

wir-form	**Gehen wir** jetzt!	*Let's go now.*
	Sprechen wir Deutsch!	*Let's speak German.*

< < What is the Subjunctive? > >

The **subjunctive** is the mood of the verb which is used to express actions that are unreal, actions that are not actual fact. Notice the difference between the indicative mood (used to express facts) and the subjunctive mood in the following examples:

Indicative

- States a fact

John *is* here.

- States something that can be a fact

    If John *is* here, you can meet him.

    Implication: There is the possibility that John is here.

Subjunctive

- States something that is contrary-to-fact

    If John *were* here, you could meet him.

    Implication: John is not here, and you cannot meet him.

    I wish John *were* here.

    Implication: But he is not.

In English: The subjunctive is difficult to recognize because it resembles tenses in the indicative. But the subjunctive does exist and you often use it without realizing it. Because the subjunctive is most readily recognizable in the verb *to be*, we will use the verb *to be* to illustrate the difference between the indicative and the subjunctive in the sentences below:

- I *am* in Europe right now.
  indicative

  I wish I *were* in Europe right now.
  subjunctive

- Mary *is* intelligent.
  indicative

  If Mary *were* intelligent, she would learn faster.
  subjunctive

The subjunctive occurs most commonly in three kinds of sentences:

1. Conditions **contrary-to-fact**, usually using *if*, called the ***if*-condition clause**

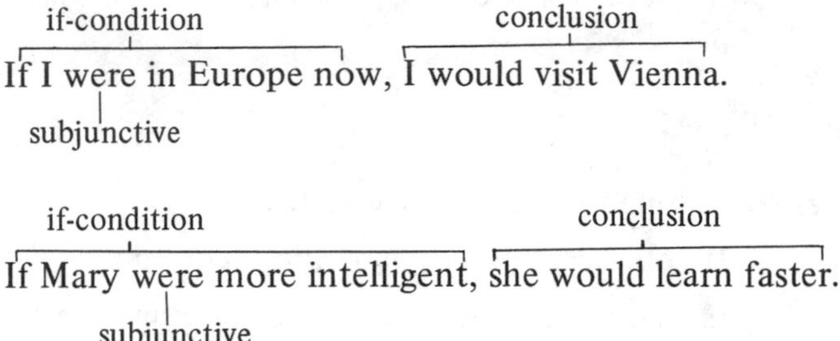

2. Expressions of wish

I wish I *were* in Europe right now.
subjunctive

If only Mary *were* more intelligent.
subjunctive

3. Expressions of necessity or demand, often with verbs of asking, urging, demanding, requesting. This use, however, requires a different form of the subjunctive, which will be discussed briefly below.

It is necessary that he *be* here.
subjunctive

I asked that she *be* present.
subjunctive

As you can see from the above examples using the verb *to be*, there are two separate forms of subjunctive in English; both have different uses:

1. Expressions contrary-to-fact and wishes

- *to be* - The **present subjunctive** is derived from the *simple past tense indicative*. Only in the subjunctive do we use the form *were* with the subjects *I*, *he/she* or *it*.

Simple past Indicative	Present Subjunctive
I was	I ***were***
you were	you were
he was	he ***were***
she was	she ***were***
it was	it ***were***
we were	we were
you were	you were
they were	they were

I *was* in Europe last year.
fact
simple past indicative

I wish I *were* in Europe.
contrary-to-fact
present subjunctive

She *was* in school when I came.
fact
simple past indicative

I wish she *were* in school.
contrary-to-fact
present subjunctive

- all other verbs – The **present subjunctive** is identical to the *simple past indicative* in all persons.

When I was young, I *spoke* German.
fact
simple past indicative

I wish I *spoke* German better.
contrary-to-fact
present subjunctive

Years ago he *understood* the language well.
fact
simple past indicative

If only he *understood* the language.
contrary-to-fact
present subjunctive

2. Expressions of necessity or demand

- The **present subjunctive** is identical to the *dictionary form* of the verb.

He *appears* promptly at noon.
fact
present indicative

It is necessary that he *appear* promptly at noon.
necessity
present subjunctive
(infinitive: *to appear*)

She *comes* to see me every week.
fact
present indicative

I asked that she *come* to see me every week.
demand
present subjunctive
(infinitive: *to come*)

In German: German subjunctive forms are much easier to identify than English ones, because the German subjunctive forms are less frequently identical to German indicative forms. As in English there are two different types of subjunctives, one derived from the simple past of the verb and one derived from the infinitive. However, in usage these two forms do not overlap with the two forms of the English subjunctive. In this section we shall discuss only one of the two types of German subjunctive, the so-called **general subjunctive** or **subjunctive II**. The other, less common, type of subjunctive is discussed in the section **What is Meant by Direct and Indirect Discourse?**, p. 88.

The general subjunctive is used commonly in two kinds of sentences:

1. Expressions contrary-to-fact

The general subjunctive is used not only in the *if*-condition (as in English), but also in the conclusion.[1]

- Wenn sie hier **wäre**, dann **wäre** ich glücklich.
subjunctive subjunctive

If she **were** *here, I would be happy.*
subjunctive

[1] See p. 84 for a discussion of this German use of the subjunctive and its English equivalent, which is not a subjunctive.

- Wenn Mary intelligenter **wäre**, dann **lernte** sie schneller.
  subjunctive subjunctive

  *If Mary **were** more intelligent, she would learn faster.*
  subjunctive

2. Expressions of wish

   The general subjunctive is used not only in the conclusion of the *wish*-statement (as in English), but the verb *wish* itself is in the subjunctive.

- Wenn sie doch nur hier **wäre!**
  subjunctive

  *If only she **were** here!*
  subjunctive

- Ich **wünschte**, ich **wäre** jetzt in Europa!
  subjunctive subjunctive

  *I wish I **were** in Europe now!*

The German subjunctive has both a present and a past tense. The present tense is formed by adding a special set of endings to the stem of the simple past indicative. The past is a compound tense and resembles the German past perfect, except that the auxiliary verb (**haben** or **sein**) is in the subjunctive rather than in the indicative. See your German textbook for a detailed explanation of these forms.

The conditional

In English: There is another verb form used instead of or together with the subjunctive in English. This is the construction using *would* + **the dictionary form of the verb**. It is sometimes called the **conditional**.

The conditional is used

- in the conclusion of an *if*- condition clause

If John *were* here, I *would be* happy.
subjunctive — conditional

If Mary *were* more intelligent, she *would learn* faster.
subjunctive — conditional

If they *visited* us, we *would entertain* them royally.
subjunctive — conditional

- in expressions of wish involving the future

I wish you *would work* harder.
conditional

If only he *would learn* to write legibly.
conditional

- in polite requests

Would you please *open* the door.
Would you *answer* this letter.

The **past conditional**, *would have* **+ verb**, is used in the conclusion of an *if*-condition clause when the verb in the *if*-clause is in the past subjunctive:

If he *had been* here, I *would have been* happy.
past subjunctive — past conditional

If the rain *had stopped*, we *would have taken* a walk.
past subjunctive — past conditional

In German: There is a conditional formed by the **present general subjunctive of *werden*** (literally *to become*) **+ the infinitive.** Note that both in English and in German the conditional form has a structure similar to the future indicative (see **What is the Future tense?**, p. 73).

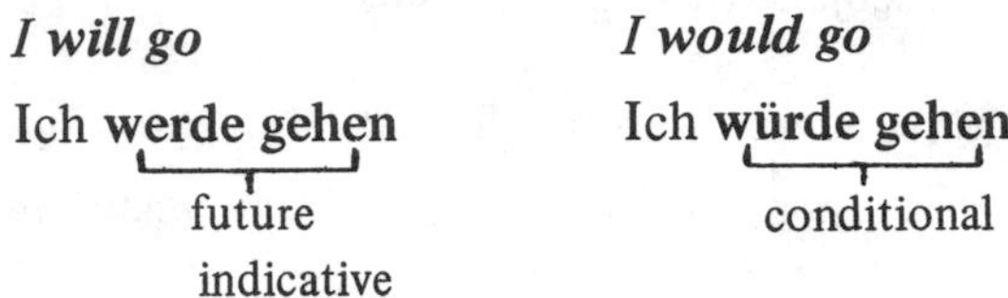

The German conditional is used

- in polite requests

Würden Sie bitte die Tür **aufmachen.**
***Would** you please **open** the door.*

Würdest du mir einen Gefallen **tun.**
***Would** you **do** me a favor.*

- as an alternative to the subjunctive in the conclusion of a *wish*-clause

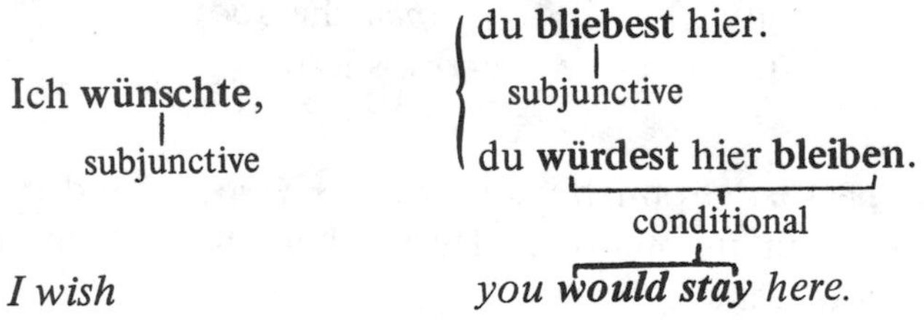

- as an alternative to the subjunctive in the conclusion of an *if*-condition clause. (Your German textbook will explain where the conditional must be used in the conclusion of *if*-conditions.)

Wenn John hier **wäre,** dann **wäre** ich glücklich.

subjunctive — subjunctive

dann **würde** ich glücklich **sein.**

conditional

*If John **were** here, then I **would be** happy.*

subjunctive — conditional

Although there is a past conditional in German, the **past subjunctive** is often used instead. You should remember this when trying to express the English *would have* + **verb** in German.

*If John **had been** here, I **would have been** happy.*

past subjunctive — past conditional

Wenn John hier **gewesen wäre,** dann

past subjunctive

wäre ich glücklich **gewesen.**

past subjunctive

There are various other situations where the subjunctive is used in German. Although its use does not always resemble that of the English subjunctive, being aware of the subjunctive in English can often help you know how to use it in German.

< < What is Meant by Direct and Indirect Discourse? > >

Direct discourse is the transmission of another person's statement or message by direct quotation. Direct discourse is set in quotation marks.

> Mary said, "I am going to Berlin."
> John asked, "What will you do in Berlin?"

Indirect discourse is the transmission of another person's statement or message without quoting his words directly. Indirect discourse reproduces the substance of the message but does not use quotation marks. Furthermore, it changes the speaker's first-person pronoun to agree logically with the perspective of the person doing the quoting.

> Mary said she was going to Berlin.
> John asked what she would do in Berlin.

In English: Indirect discourse is often indicated by a shift in tense.

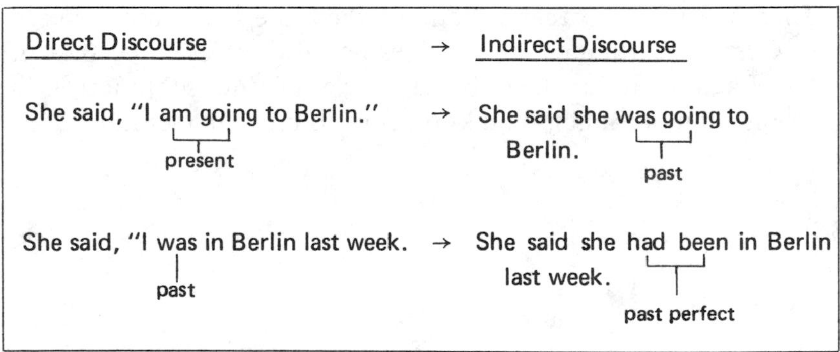

In German: Indirect discourse is indicated by a shift in mood from the indicative to the subjunctive. There is a special subjunctive called the **indirect discourse subjunctive** or **subjunctive I**; it is used primarily for indirect discourse in writing. In conversation the general subjunctive is often used for indirect discourse.

Direct Discourse	→	Indirect Discourse
Mary sagte, "**Ich fahre** nach Berlin." present indicative	→	Mary sagte, **sie fahre** nach Berlin. special subjunctive present Mary sagte, **sie führe** nach Berlin. general subjunctive present
Mary said, "**I am going** *to Berlin.*"	→	*Mary said* **she was going** *to Berlin.*
Mary sagte, "**Ich war** in Berlin." simple past indicative	→	Mary sagte, **sie sei** in Berlin special subjunctive past **gewesen.** Mary sagte, **sie wäre** in Berlin general subjunctive past **gewesen.**
Mary said, "**I was** *in Berlin.*"	→	*Mary said* **she had been** *in Berlin.*

The **present tense** of the special subjunctive is **the infinitive stem + the subjunctive endings**. The **past tense** is *haben* or *sein* in the **present of the special subjunctive + the past participle**.

Your German textbook will explain in greater detail the formation and use of the special indirect discourse subjunctive.

<< What is a Possessive Pronoun? >>

A **possessive pronoun** is a word which replaces a noun and which also shows who possesses that noun.

> Whose house is that?
> *Mine.*

Mine is a pronoun which replaces the noun *house* and which shows who possesses that noun.

In English: Possessive pronouns refer only to the person who possesses, not to the object possessed.

> Example 1. Is that your house? Yes, it is *mine*.
>
> Example 2. Are those your keys? Yes, they are *mine*.

The same possessive pronoun *mine* is used, although the object possessed is singular in Example 1 (*house*) and plural in Example 2 (*keys*).

Here is a list of the English possessive pronouns:

mine	ours
yours	yours
his, hers, its	theirs

The possessive pronoun refers to the person who possesses.

> John's car is blue. *His* is blue.
>
> Mary's car is green. *Hers* is green.

In German: The forms of the possessive pronouns are essentially the same as those of the possessive adjectives (see **What is a Possessive Adjective?**, p. 123). Only the endings are different. As adjectives these words use the same endings as the indefinite article (**ein, eine, ein**). As pronouns they use the same endings as the definite article (**der, die, das**).

Possessive adjective	Possessive pronoun
Das ist **mein** Buch.	Das ist *meins*.
*That is **my** book.*	(neuter singular nominative ending *das*)
	*That is **mine**.*
Hier ist **unser** Bleistift.	Hier ist *unserer*.
*Here is **our** pencil.*	(masculine singular nominative ending *der*)
	*Here is **ours**.*

<< What is a Reflexive Pronoun? >>

A **reflexive pronoun** is a pronoun which is used either as the object of a verb or as the object of a preposition and which refers back to the subject of the sentence: it *reflects* the meaning back to the subject.

In English: Reflexive pronouns end with *-self* in the singular and *-selves* in the plural:

myself	ourselves
yourself	yourselves
himself	themselves
herself	
itself	

Observe their usage:

1. as object of a verb

- I cut *myself* with the knife.
  subject direct object

  Who cut himself with the knife? I.
  I is the subject of the sentence.

  Whom did I cut with the knife? Myself.
  Myself is the direct object of the verb *cut*.

- I can't help *myself*.
  subject direct object.

  Who can't help himself? I.
  I is the subject of the sentence.

  Whom can I not help? Myself.
  Myself is the direct object of the verb *help*.

- You should write *yourself* a note.
  subject indirect object

  Who should write himself a note? You.
  You is the subject of the sentence.

  To whom should you write a note? To yourself.
  Yourself is the indirect object of the verb *write*.

  What should you write yourself? A note.
  Note is the direct object of the verb *write*.

2. as object of a preposition

- He thinks only of *himself*.
  subject object of preposition

Who thinks only of himself? He.
He is the subject of the sentence.

Of whom does he think? Of himself.
Himself is the object of the preposition *of*.

- You talk about *yourself* too much.

subject — object of preposition

Who spoke about himself? You.
You is the subject of the sentence.

About whom did you speak? About yourself.
Yourself is the object of the preposition *about*.

In German: As in English there are reflexive pronouns for each of the different personal pronouns (1st, 2nd, and 3rd persons). However, the German reflexive pronouns will have both an accusative form (for direct objects and for prepositions that require the accusative) and a dative form (for indirect objects and for prepositions that require the dative). Depending on the verb or the preposition, you will choose either the accusative reflexive pronoun or the dative reflexive pronoun.

Nominative subject pronoun	Accusative reflexive pronoun	Dative reflexive pronoun	
ich	mich	mir	*myself*
du	dich	dir	*yourself*
er/sie/es	sich	sich	*himself* *herself* *itself*
wir	uns	uns	*ourselves*
ihr	euch	euch	*yourselves*
sie/Sie	sich	sich	*themselves*

If you compare this table of accusative and dative reflexive pronouns with the table of accusative and dative personal pronouns (p. 39), you will see that they differ only in three persons:

third person singular
third person plural
second person formal

A single form, **sich**, is used as the reflexive pronoun for all of these persons.

Like English reflexive pronouns, German reflexive pronouns are used as objects of verbs and as objects of prepositions. In both instances you will need to pay attention to the case required.

1. as object of a verb

- *I cut **myself** with the knife.*

  Ich habe **mich** mit dem Messer geschnitten.
  subject — accusative object of **habe geschnitten**

- *I can't help **myself**.*

  Ich kann **mir** nicht helfen.
  subject — dative object of **helfen**

  Remember: **Helfen** is a verb that requires a dative object.

- *You should write **yourself** a note.*

  Du solltest **dir** einen Zettel schreiben.
  subject — dative object — accusative object

  Schreiben, like its English equivalent *to write*, can take two objects.

2. as object of a preposition

- *He thinks only of* ***himself****.*

  Er denkt nur an **sich**.

  subject — accusative object of **denken an**

- *You talk about* ***yourself*** *too much.*

  Du redest zuviel von **dir**.

  subject — dative object of **von**

<< What is a Reflexive Verb? >>

A **reflexive verb** is a verb conjugated with a reflexive pronoun.

In English: There are no verbs which require a reflexive pronoun in order to complete their meaning. The verbs which can have a reflexive pronoun as their object can also have other nouns or pronouns as their object.

I hurt *myself*.
reflexive pronoun as direct object

I don't like to hurt *people*.
noun as direct object

Please, calm *yourself*.
reflexive pronoun as direct object

The soft music calmed his *nerves*.
noun as direct object

In German: There are some verbs that are used only with reflexive pronouns. These verbs are called **reflexive verbs**. The English equivalents of these verbs do not have reflexive pronouns:

sich erholen	*to recover*
sich befinden	*to be located*
sich verlieben	*to fall in love*

As you can see, the infinitive of these verbs is always given with the third person reflexive pronoun, **sich**. When you conjugate a reflexive verb, you will need to change the reflexive pronoun as you change the subject. Here is the verb **sich erholen** (*to recover*) conjugated in the present tense. Notice that this verb takes the accusative form of the reflexive pronoun.

Subject pronoun	Verb	Reflexive pronoun
ich	erhole	mich
du	erholst	dich
er	erholt	sich
sie	erholt	sich
es	erholt	sich
wir	erholen	uns
ihr	erholt	euch
sie	erholen	sich
Sie	erholen	sich

Reflexive verbs can be conjugated in all tenses. The subject pronoun and reflexive pronoun remain the same regardless of the verb tense:

du **erholst** dich — *you are recovering*
(present)

du **wirst** dich **erholen** — *you will recover*
(future)

du **hast** dich **erholt** — *you recovered*
(hast ... erholt: perfect)

As you learn new vocabulary, you will need to memorize which German verbs are reflexive, that is, which ones require the reflexive pronoun as part of the whole verb.

<< What is an Interrogative Pronoun? >>

An **interrogative pronoun** is a pronoun (a word used in place of a noun) which introduces a question; *interrogative* is related to *interrogate*, meaning *to question.*

In English: Different interrogative pronouns are used for asking about persons and for asking about things:

What is on the table?[1]	refers to a thing
Who is in the room?	refers to a person

The personal interrogative pronoun, like some of the personal pronouns in English, has different case forms. (See **What is a Personal Pronoun?**, p. 33.)

---

[1] Do not confuse with "*What* book is on the table?" where *what* is an interrogative adjective. See p. 125.

- ***Who*** is the nominative form and is used for the subject of the sentence:

  Who wrote that book?
  subject — direct object

  Who lives here?
  subject

  Who will help you?
  subject — direct object

- ***Whom*** is the objective form and is used for the direct object of the sentence and, in standard written English, for the object of a preposition (See **What are Objects?**, p. 20).

  Whom do you know here?
  direct object — subject

  From *whom* did you get the book?
  preposition — object of preposition — subject

In spoken or colloquial English we often use the nominative case *who* instead of the objective case *whom*. In colloquial English the two sentences above would be as follows:

Who do you know here?
Who did you get the book from?

- ***Whose*** is the possessive form and is used to ask about possession or ownership:

  I found a pencil. *Whose* is it?
  I have Mary's paper. *Whose* do you have?

In German: As in English, different interrogative pronouns are used for asking about persons and for asking about things. Let us look at the interrogative pronouns referring to persons first because they are more complicated.

- a person

  You will have to determine the proper case form. To do this, you must recognize the pronoun's function in the sentence.

  1. Is it the subject of the question?
  2. Is it the direct object of the verb?
     Does that verb take the accusative or the dative?
  3. Is it the indirect object of the verb?
  4. Is it the object of a preposition?
     Does that preposition take the accusative or the dative?
  5. Is it a possessive pronoun?

1. ***who*** (subject) = **wer** (nominative)

- ***Who** is in the room*?

  Function of *who*: subject of *is*
  Case in German: nominative

  Wer ist im Zimmer?

- ***Who** is coming this evening?*
  Hans and Inge are coming.

  Function of *who*: subject of *is coming*
  Case in German: nominative

Wer kommt heute abend?
Hans und Inge kommen.

2. ***who(m)*** (direct object) = **wen** (accusative) usually
wem (dative) occasionally

The interrogative pronoun used as an object is harder for you to identify because the *whom* form, which is the correct form, has been replaced by *who* in much everyday language. You will, therefore, have to analyze the sentence carefully to find the grammatical function of *who(m)*.

- ***Who** do you see*?

Function of *who*: direct object of *see*
You is the subject of *see*.
Case: German verb **sehen** (*to see*) requires an accusative object.

Wen sehen Sie?

- ***Who** is Peter visiting*?

Function of *who*: direct object of *is visiting*
Case: German verb **besuchen** (*to visit*) requires an accusative object.

Wen besucht Peter?

- ***Who** are they helping?*

Function of *who*: direct object of *are helping*
They is the subject of *are helping*.
Case: German verb **helfen** (*to help*) requires a dative object.

Wem helfen sie?

- ***Who** can I believe?*

Function of *who*: direct object of *can believe*
Case: German verb **glauben** (*to believe*) requires a dative personal object.

Wem kann ich glauben?

3. ***who(m)*** (indirect object) = **wem** (dative)

- ***Who** is she sending a letter to?*[1]

Who is she sending a letter *to*?	→	*To whom* is she sending a letter?

Function of *who*: indirect object of *is sending*
She is the subject of *is sending.*
A letter is the direct object.
Case: dative

Wem schickt sie einen Brief?

- ***Who** did you tell the story to?*[1]

Who did you tell the story *to*?	→	*To whom* did you tell the story?

Function of *who*: indirect object of *did tell*
You is the subject of *did tell.*
The story is the direct object.
Case: dative

Wem hast du die Geschichte erzählt?

[1] Remember to restructure the dangling preposition. See. p. 134.

4. ***who(m)*** (object of a preposition) =
preposition + **wen** (accusative)
preposition + **wem** (dative)

- ***Who** is he talking about?*[1]

Who is he talking *about*?	→	*About whom* is he talking?

Function of *who*: object of preposition
He is the subject of *is talking.*
Case: **Von** (*about*) requires a dative object.

Von wem spricht er?

- ***Who** are we going with?*[1]

Who are we going *with*?	→	*With whom* are we going?

Function of *who*: object of preposition
We is the subject of *are going*.
Case: **Mit** (*with*) requires a dative object.

Mit wem gehen wir?

- ***Who** are you doing that for?*[1]

Who are you doing that *for*?	→	*For whom* are you doing that?

Function of *who:* object of preposition
You is the subject of *are doing.*
Case: **Für** (*for*) requires an accusative object.

Für wen machst du das?

---

[1] Remember to restructure the dangling preposition. See. p. 134.

• ***Who*** *is she waiting for?*[1]

Who is she waiting *for*? → *For whom* is she waiting?

Function of *who*: object of preposition
She is the subject of *is waiting.*
Case: **Warten auf** (*to wait for*) requires an accusative object.

Auf wen wartet sie?

5. ***whose*** (possessive) = **wessen** (genitive)

This form should present no problems since the English form *whose* can be identified easily and there is only one form in German.

Whose *pencil is that?*
Wessen Bleistift ist das?

Whose *house did you buy?*
Wessen Haus habt ihr gekauft?

• a thing

There is only one interrogative pronoun for asking about things; the German equivalent of *what* is **was**. The same form is used for the nominative, dative, and accusative cases, and no distinction is made between the singular and the plural.

[1] Remember to restructure the dangling preposition. See. p. 134.

What *is in this package?*
subject

Was ist in diesem Paket?
nominative

What *are you doing?*
direct object subject

Was machst du?
accusative

What *did he talk about?*[1]
object of preposition (*About what* did he talk?)

Von **was** hat er geredet?[2]
dative with **von**

What *is that used for?*[1]
object of preposition (*For what* is that used?)

Für **was** wird das verwendet?[2]
accusative with **für**

---

[1] Remember to restructure the dangling preposition, see p. 134.

[2] The ***wo*-compounds** are another way of asking about a thing which is the object of a preposition: "**Wovon** hat er geredet?" "**Wofür** wird das verwendet?" See your German textbook for more information on wo-compounds.

< < What is a Relative Pronoun? > >

A **relative pronoun** is a word that serves two purposes:

1. As a pronoun it stands for a noun or another pronoun previously mentioned (called its **antecedent**).

   This is the boy ***who*** broke the window.

   antecedent

2. It introduces a **subordinate clause**, that is, a group of words having a subject and verb separate from the main subject and verb of the sentence. (See **What is a Clause**?, p. 154.)

   This is the boy ***who*** broke the window.

   main clause — subordinate clause

   The above subordinate clause is also called a **relative clause** because it starts with a relative pronoun (*who*). A relative pronoun relates the subordinate clause to its antecedent (*boy*).

In English and in German, the relative pronoun used will depend on the function of the relative pronoun in the relative clause. You must train yourself to go through the following steps:

1. Find the relative clause.

2. Determine the function of the relative pronoun in the relative clause.
   - Is it the subject?
   - Is it the direct object?
   - Is it the indirect object?
   - Is it an object of a preposition?
   - Is it a possessive modifier?

3. Select the proper relative pronoun based on steps 1 and 2.

In English: Here are the English relative pronouns.

Subject of the relative clause:

- ***who*** (if the antecedent is a person)

  This is the student *who* answered.
  antecedent

  Who is the subject of *answered.*

- ***which*** (if the antecedent is a thing)

  This is the book *which* is so popular.
  antecedent

  Which is the subject of *is.*

- ***that*** (if the antecedent is a thing)

  This is the book *that* is so popular.
  antecedent

  That is the subject of *is.*

Object of the relative clause: These pronouns are often omitted in English. We have indicated them in parentheses because they must be expressed in German.

- ***whom*** (if the antecedent is a person)

  This is the student (*whom*) I saw.
  antecedent — subject of relative clause

  Whom is the direct object of *saw.*

- ***which*** (if the antecedent is a thing)

  This is the book (*which*) I bought.
  antecedent — subject of relative clause

  Which is the direct object of *bought*.

- ***that*** (if the antecedent is a thing)

  This is the book (*that*) I read.
  antecedent — subject of relative clause

  That is the direct object of *read*.

Possessive modifier

- ***whose*** (if the antecedent is a person)

  Here is the woman *whose* car was stolen.
  antecedent — possessive modifying *car*

Only the relative pronoun for persons shows different case forms in English: *who* (nominative), *whom* (objective), and *whose* (possessive).

These relative pronouns enable you to combine two sentences into one. Look at the following examples:

- Sentence A: That is the boy.
  Sentence B: He broke the window.

  You can combine Sentence A and Sentence B by replacing the subject pronoun *he* with the relative pronoun *who*.

  That is the boy *who broke the window*.

Who broke the window is the **relative clause.** It does not express a complete thought and it is introduced by a relative pronoun.

Who stands for the noun *boy*. *Boy* is called the **antecedent** of *who*. Notice that the antecedent stands immediately before the pronoun which gives additional information about it.

Who serves as the subject of the verb *broke* in the relative clause *who broke the window*.

- Sentence A: The German teacher is nice.
  Sentence B: I met her today.

You can combine Sentence A and Sentence B by replacing the object pronoun *her* with the relative pronoun *whom*.

The German teacher, *whom I met today*, is nice.

Whom I met today is the relative clause.

Whom stands for the noun *teacher*. *Teacher* is the antecedent. Notice again that the antecedent comes immediately before the relative pronoun.

Whom serves as the direct object of the relative clause. ("*I*" is the subject.)

- Sentence A: Here is the student.
  Sentence B: I am speaking about him.

You can combine Sentence A and Sentence B by replacing the preposition + personal pronoun (*about him*) with the preposition + relative pronoun (*about whom*).

In spoken English, you would combine these two sentences by saying, "Here is the student I am speaking about." To say this in German, you will need to change the structure.

Take the preposition *about* from the end of the sentence (a preposition separated from its object is called a **dangling preposition**, see p. 134) and use it to begin the relative clause. Put it right at the place where you will connect the two sentences. Then you will need to add the relative pronoun *whom* right after the preposition *about*:

Here is the student I am speaking *about*.	→	Here is the student *about whom* I am speaking.

Restructuring English sentences which contain a dangling preposition will help you identify the relative clause and will give you the first step toward determining correct German word order.

John is the boy I'm going *with*.	→	John is the boy *with whom* I am going.
The girls I'm writing *to* live in Munich.	→	The girls *to whom* I'm writing live in Munich.

In German: There are case forms for relative pronouns in all four cases, depending on the function of the relative pronoun in the relative clause (nominative, genitive, dative, and accusative). In German, it does not matter whether the antecedent is a person or a thing: the same set of relative pronouns refers to both. What is important is the gender and number of the antecedent: this will determine the gender and the number of the relative pronoun. The various forms of the relative pronoun are very similar to the forms of the definite article (**der, die, das**). Look at your German textbook to learn these forms.

NOTE: Although the relative pronouns **who, whom, that,** and **which** are often omitted in English, they must always be stated in German.

In English: We can say either:

1. Is that the house *that* Jack built?

   or

2. Is that the house Jack built?

1. Is there anyone here *who(m)* you know?

   or

2. Is there anyone here you know?

In German: Since the relative pronoun can never be omitted, only sentence 1 would be possible.

To find the correct relative pronoun in German you must go through the following steps:

1. Recognize the relative clause; restructure the English clause if there is a dangling preposition.[1]
2. Find the antecedent: what word in the main clause does the relative clause relate to?
3. Determine the number and gender of the antecedent.
   - Is it singular or plural?
   - If it is singular, is it masculine, feminine, or neuter?
4. Determine the function and therefore the case of the relative pronoun within the relative clause:

	Case
• Is it the subject?	nominative
• Is it a direct object?	accusative (usually)
• Is it an indirect object?	dative

[1] See p. 134.

- Is it the object of a preposition?
  What case does the preposition take? — accusative / dative / genitive
- Is it a possessive modifier? — genitive

5. Select the proper form based on steps 1-4.

Let us apply the steps outlined above to the following sentences in order to select the correct relative pronoun:

- *The man* ***who*** *visted us was nice.*

  1. Relative clause: *who visited us*
  2. Antecedent: *man*
  3. Number and gender of antecedent: **Der Mann** is masculine singular.
  4. Function of *who* within relative clause: subject = nominative
  5. Selection: masculine singular nominative → **der**

  Der Mann, **der** uns besuchte, war nett.

- *Is that the bike you bought?*

  1. Relative clause: *(that) you bought*
     Remember that the relative pronoun must always be stated in German.
  2. Antecedent: *the bike*
  3. Number and gender of antecedent: **Das Rad** is neuter singular.
  4. Function of (*that*) within relative clause: direct object = accusative
  5. Selection: neuter singular accusative → **das**

  Ist das das Rad, **das** du gekauft hast?

---

[1] Remember to restructure the dangling preposition. See p. 134.

- *Hans, **whose** alarm clock was broken, overslept.*

  1. Relative clause: *whose alarm clock was broken*
  2. Antecedent: *Hans*
  3. Number and gender of antecedent: Since *Hans* is the name of one man or boy, it is masculine singular.
  4. Function of *whose* within relative clause: possessive modifier connecting *Hans* with his *alarm clock* = genitive
  5. Selection: masculine singular genitive → **dessen**

  Hans, **dessen** Wecker kaputt war, hat sich verschlafen.

- *Where is the woman you went to the movies with?*[1]

Where is the woman you went to the movies *with*?	→	Where is the woman *with whom* you went to the movies?

  1. Relative clause: *with whom you went to the movies*
  2. Antecedent: *woman*
  3. Number and gender of antecedent: **Die Frau** is feminine singular.
  4. Function of *who* within relative clause: object of preposition *with*. **Mit** always takes a dative object.
  5. Selection: feminine singular dative → **der**

  Wo ist die Frau, **mit der** du ins Kino gegangen bist?

- *Here are those books you were talking about.*[1]

Here are those books you were talking *about*.	→	Here are those books *about which* you were talking.

  1. Relative clause: *about which you were talking*
  2. Antecedent: *books*
  3. Number and gender of antecedent: **Die Bücher** is (neuter) plural.
     (With plurals the gender is not important, because there is only one set of plural forms for all three genders.)

---

[1] Remember to restructure the dangling preposition. See. p. 134.

4. Function of *which* within relative clause: object of preposition *about.* **Von** always takes a dative object.
5. Selection: neuter plural dative → **denen**

Hier sind die Bücher, **von denen** Sie geredet haben.

Relative pronouns are difficult to handle, and this handbook provides only a simple outline. Refer to your German textbook for further help.

Relative clauses with indefinite antecedents

In all of the above examples, a particular noun or pronoun in the main clause can clearly be identified as the antecedent of the relative clause. When no such single antecedent is clearly apparent, the relative clause is said to have an indefinite antecedent.

In English: We avoid using a relative pronoun which does not have a definite antecedent, especially in standard written English.

Hans invited us all, which we found nice.
main clause — relative clause

Here is a relative clause, but there is no clear antecedent. The relative clause can be said to refer to the entire idea expressed in the main clause. In English we avoid such sentences, rewriting them in other ways:

We found it nice that Hans invited us all.

In German: It is perfectly acceptable to consider an entire clause as the antecedent of the relative clause. In such sentences the same relative pronoun is always used: **was**.

Hans invited us all, ***which*** *we found nice.*
main clause — relative clause

Hans hat uns alle eingeladen, **was** wir nett gefunden haben.
entire clause as antecedent — relative pronoun

There are other instances in German which require the use of **was** as a relative pronoun. Consult your German textbook.

NOTE: The punctuation of English relative clauses reflects a distinction between those clauses which are "restrictive" and those which are "non-restrictive."

1. **Restrictive clause**–A clause that restricts or limits the meaning of the antecedent; such a clause is essential to the meaning of the sentence and cannot be omitted without changing the sense of the whole sentence. It is not set off from the rest of the sentence by commas. A restrictive clause is introduced by *who, whom, whose, which,* or *that.*

   Do you know the girl *who* won the prize?
   antecedent — relative clause

   The relative clause is essential to identify the antecedent, *the girl.* Thus the clause is restrictive and is not set off by commas.

2. **Non-restrictive clause**–A clause that is not essential to the meaning of the sentence and which could be omitted without losing any of the meaning. It is set off from the rest of the sentence by commas. A non-restrictive clause is introduced by *who, whom, whose,* or *which*; the relative pronoun *that* cannot introduce a non-restrictive clause.

My friend John, *whom* you met last week, is here.

antecedent relative clause

The relative clause is not essential to identify the antecedent; it merely gives additional information about *my friend John*. Thus the clause is non-restrictive and must be set off by commas.

Often in your own writing you can decide only from the context of the sentence whether a relative clause in it is restrictive or non-restrictive. German does not have this distinction: all German relative clauses are separated from the main clause by commas.

< < What is an Adjective? > >

An **adjective** is a word that describes a noun or a pronoun. Be sure that you do not confuse an adjective with a pronoun. A pronoun replaces a noun, while an adjective must always have a noun or a pronoun to describe.

In English: Adjectives describe nouns in many ways. They can tell:

- ***what kind*** of noun it is – **descriptive adjective**

  The house was *large*.
  The woman is *intelligent*.
  The *small* child plays in front of the *red* house.

- ***whose*** noun it is – **possessive adjective**

  His book is lost.
  Our parents are away.

- *which* noun is it? – **interrogative adjective**

  What book is lost?

  Which newspaper do you want?

- *which* noun it is – **demonstrative adjective**

  This teacher is excellent.

  That question is very appropriate.

In all these cases, it is said that the adjective *modifies* the noun.

In German: Adjectives are identified in the same way as in English. It is important to recognize two different uses of German descriptive adjectives:

1. **Attributive adjectives**—are adjectives which appear before the noun they modify.

   the small child
   small: attributive adjective

   the red house
   red: attributive adjective

   Attributive adjectives in German have special endings according to the gender, number, and case of the noun they modify, and according to whether they are preceded by an indefinite article, a definite article, or by no article at all. Your German textbook will show you these endings, and you must memorize them until you can use the correct one automatically.

   - ***The small** child plays in front of **the red** house.*

     Das kleine Kind spielt vor **dem roten** Haus.

     Das kleine: definite article + adjective, neuter nominative singular

     dem roten: definite article + adjective, neuter dative singular

- *A **small** child plays in front of **a red** house.*

  Ein kleines Kind spielt vor **einem roten** Haus.

  indefinite article + adjective / neuter nominative singular (Ein kleines)

  indefinite article + adjective / neuter dative singular (einem roten)

- ***The old** wine was expensive.*

  Der alte Wein war teuer.

  definite article + adjective
  masculine nominative singular

- ***Old** wine is expensive.*

  Alter Wein ist teuer.

  adjective without article
  masculine nominative singular

2. **Predicate adjectives**—are adjectives which accompany a linking verb (see **What is a Predicate Noun?**, p. 26), often a form of the verb *to be*. Predicate adjectives modify the subject of the sentence.

- The child is small.

  subject (The child) — linking verb (is) — predicate adjective (small)

- The house is red.

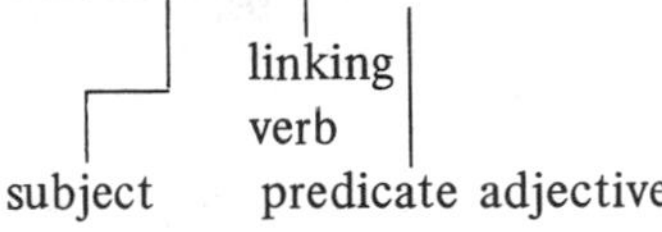

- I am getting tired.

  subject (I) — linking verb (am getting) — predicate adjective (tired)

In German these predicate adjectives never have special adjective endings like those found on attributive adjectives.

- *The child is **small.***

  Das Kind ist **klein.**

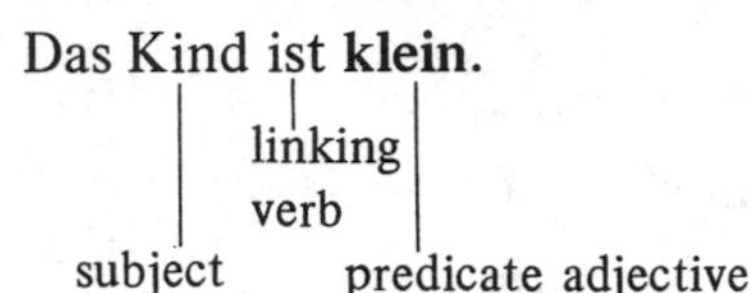

- *The house is **red.***

  Das Haus ist **rot.**

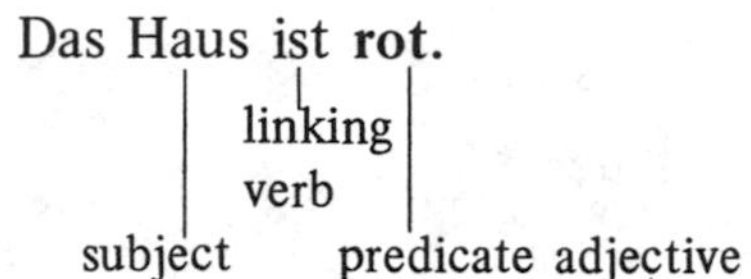

- *I am getting **tired.***

  Ich werde **müde.**

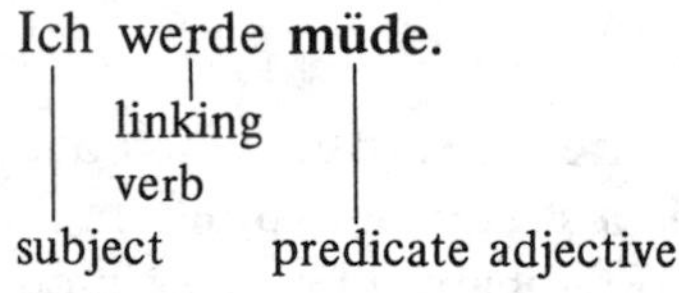

< < What is Meant by Comparison of Adjectives? > >

When adjectives are used to compare the qualities of the nouns they modify, they change forms. This change is called **comparison.**

comparison of adjectives

John is tall but Anthony is taller.

adjective modifying the noun *John* — adjective modifying the noun *Anthony*

There are three degrees of comparison: **positive**, **comparative** and **superlative**.

In English: Let us go over what is meant by the different degrees of comparison and how each degree is formed.

1. The positive form refers to the quality of one person or thing. It is simply the adjective form.

   Mary is *pretty.*
   My house is *big.*
   His car is *expensive.*
   This book is *interesting.*

2. The comparative form compares the quality of one person or thing with another person or thing. It is formed:

   - by adding ***-er*** to short adjectives.

     Mary is *prettier* than Ann.
     My house is *bigger* than his.

   - by placing ***more*** in front of longer adjectives.

     His car is *more expensive* than mine.
     This book is *more interesting* than that one.

3. The superlative form is used to stress the highest degree of a quality. It is formed:

   - by adding ***-est*** to short adjectives.

     Mary is the *prettiest* in the family.
     My house is the *biggest* on the street.

   - by placing ***the most*** in front of longer adjectives.

     His car is *the most expensive* in the race.
     This book is *the most interesting* of all.

A few adjectives do not follow this regular pattern of comparison. You must use an entirely different word for the comparative and the superlative.

This apple is bad.	(positive)
This apple is worse. not "badder"	(comparative)
This apple is the worst. not "baddest"	(superlative)

In German: Comparisons of adjectives have the same three degrees as in English.

1. The positive is simply the dictionary form of the adjective.

   Maria ist **intelligent**.
   *Maria is **intelligent**.*

   Sein Haus ist **alt**.
   *His house is **old**.*

   Dieses Buch ist **langweilig**.
   *This book is **boring**.*

2. The comparative is formed by adding **-er** to the stem of the adjective. This form corresponds to the comparative of many short English adjectives.

> Maria ist **jünger** als ihr Bruder.
> *Maria is* ***younger*** *than her brother.*
>
> Das Buch ist **langweiliger** als der Film.
> *The book is* ***more boring*** *than the film.*

Whether the comparative adjective takes an additional ending or not depends on whether it is a predicate adjective or an attributive adjective (see **What is an Adjective?**, p. 115).

- Predicate adjective—no ending other than the **-er** of the comparative. (See examples above.)
- Attributive adjective—add *-er* + **case/gender/number ending**

Adjective stem	
jung	Ich kenne d**as** jün**gere** Mädchen nicht. neuter singular accusative *I don't know the* ***younger*** *girl.*
billig	Konntest du kein**e** billig**eren** Plätze finden? (masculine) plural accusative *Couldn't you find* ***cheaper*** *seats?*
alt	Ein ält**erer** Herr kam an die Tür. masculine singular nominative *An* ***older*** *gentleman came to the door.*

German also has several irregular comparatives just as English does:

Positive		Comparative	
gut	*good*	besser	*better*
viel	*much*	mehr	*more*

You will find a list of these irregular comparatives in your German textbook.

3. The superlative degree of the adjective is formed by adding **-st** to the adjective stem (**-est** if the adjective stem ends in **-d**, **-t**, **-z**, **-s**, or **-ss**).

   The superlative adjective is used differently if it is a predicate adjective or an attributive adjective.

   - Predicate adjective–it takes the two-word form *am* + **adjective + -st + -en**

     Inge ist **am kleinsten.**
     *Inge is **the smallest**.*

     Dieses Buch ist **am neuesten.**
     *This book is **the newest**.*

     Im Winter ist das Wetter **am kältesten.**
     *In winter the weather is (the) **coldest**.*

   - Attributive adjective–it is preceded by the definite article (**der**, **die**, **das**) and has the appropriate case/number/gender ending.

     Inge ist **das kleinste** Mädchen in der Schule.
     neuter singular nominative
     *Inge is **the smallest** girl in the school.*

Die Bücher sind alle neu, aber dieses ist **das neueste.**

neuter singular nominative

The books are all new, but this one is ***the newest.***

Das Buch is understood to be the final word in the sentence, modified by **das neueste.**

Some superlatives are irregular and will have to be memorized; the same adjectives that are irregular in the comparative are irregular in the superlative:

Positive		Superlative	
gut	*good*	am besten	*best*
viel	*much*	am meisten	*most*

<< What is a Possessive Adjective? >>

A **possessive adjective** is a word which describes a noun by showing who possesses it.

In English: Here is a list of the possessive adjectives:

my	our
your	your
his, her, its	their

The possessive adjective refers to the person who possesses.

John's mother is young. *His* mother is young.
Mary's father is rich. *Her* father is rich.
The cat's ears are short. *Its* ears are short.

In German: The possessive adjective refers to the person who possesses. The ending on the possessive adjective agrees in gender, number, and case with the noun possessed.

Here are the steps you should follow to choose the correct possessive adjective and its proper form:

1. Indicate the possessor.

	German equivalent (nominative)
my	**mein**
your (familiar singular)	**dein**
his	**sein**
her	**ihr**
its	**sein**
our	**unser**
your (familiar plural)	**euer**
their	**ihr**
your (formal)	**Ihr**

2. Identify the gender, number, and case of the noun possessed:

*He always forgets **his** books.*
Er vergißt immer sein? Bücher.

Gender:	**Buch** is neuter.
Number:	plural
Case:	direct object of **vergißt** = accusative

*She gives **her** brother **her** telephone number.*
Sie gibt ihr? Bruder ihr? Telefonnummer.

Gender:	**Bruder** is masculine.
Number:	singular
Case:	indirect object of **gibt** = dative (She gives her number *to whom*? Her brother.)

Gender:	**Telefonnummer** is feminine.
Number:	singular
Case:	direct object of **vergißt** = accusative (She gives her brother *what*? Her number.)

3. Provide the proper ending for the possessive adjective. The possessive adjectives have the same endings as the indefinite article **(ein, eine, ein)**.

Er vergißt immer **seine** Bücher.
accusative plural
he forgets always his books

Sie gibt **ihrem** Bruder **ihre** Telefonnummer.
masc. sing. dative — fem. sing. accusative
she gives her brother her telephone number

Once you have memorized the endings well, you can perform this whole process automatically.

< < What is an Interrogative Adjective? > >

An **interrogative adjective** is a word which asks a question about a noun.

In English: The words ***which*** and ***what*** are called interrogative adjectives when they come in front of a noun and are used to ask a question.

Which book do you want?
What dress do you want to wear?

In German: There is one interrogative adjective which serves as the equivalent of both of these English interrogative adjectives: **welcher**, **welche**, **welches** (in the nominative case, singular). It precedes the noun it modifies and agrees with the noun in gender, number, and case. The endings are the same as for the definite article (**der**, **die**, **das**), except that **-es** replaces **-as** in the neuter singular nominative and accusative.

- ***Which*** *book would you like?*
  Welches Buch möchtest du?
  neuter singular
  direct object of **möchtest** = accusative

- ***Which (what)*** *dress do you want to wear?*
  Welches Kleid willst du tragen?
  neuter singular
  direct object of **tragen** = accusative

- ***Which*** *man do we give our tickets to?*
  Welchem Mann geben wir unsere Karten?
  masculine singular
  indirect object of **geben** = dative
  (**Karten** is the direct object.)

If the noun functions as the object of a preposition, the word order of the question will be as follows:

preposition + interrogative adjective + noun

Make sure you restructure conversational English to formal English.

- ***Which** street does he live on?*

Which street does he live *on*?	→	*On which* street does he live?

In **welcher** Straße wohnt er?
feminine singular
object of **in** = dative

- ***What** film are you talking about?*

What film are you talking *about*?	→	*About what* film are you talking?

Von **welchem** Film sprecht ihr?
masculine singular
object of **von** = dative

< < What is an Adverb? > >

An **adverb** is a word that modifies (describes) a verb, an adjective or another adverb. Adverbs indicate quantity, time, place, intensity and manner.

Mary drives ***well.***
verb

The house is ***very*** big.
adjective

The girl ran ***too*** quickly.
adverb

In English: Here are some examples of adverbs:

- of quantity or degree

  Mary sleeps ***little***.
  Bob does well ***enough*** in class.

  These adverbs answer the question *how much* or *how well.*

- of time

  He will come ***soon***.
  The children came ***late***.

  These adverbs answer the question *when*.

- of place

  The teacher looked ***around***.
  The old were left ***behind***.

  These adverbs answer the question *where*.

- of intensity

  Bob ***really*** wants to learn Spanish.
  Mary can ***actually*** read Latin.

  These adverbs are used for *emphasis*.

- of manner

  Bob sings ***beautifully***.
  They parked the car ***carefully***.

  These adverbs answer the question *how*. They are the most common adverbs and can usually be recognized by their **-ly** ending.

Some, though not many, adverbs in English are identical in form to the corresponding adjectives:

The guests came late. (late = adverb)	We greeted the late guests. (late = adjective)
Don't drive so fast. (fast = adverb)	Fast drivers cause accidents. (Fast = adjective)
She works very hard. (hard = adverb)	This homework is hard. (hard = adjective)

In German: There is no general ending which we can add to an adjective to make it an adverb the way we often add *-ly* to adjectives in English in order to make them adverbs. Instead, German adverbs have the same form as their corresponding adjectives but without endings. They are like the small group of English adverb-adjectives above.

Adverb	Adjective
Hans fährt **schnell.** *Hans drives **fast.***	Der Wagen ist **schnell.** *The car is **fast.***
Ilse singt **schön.** *Ilse sings **beautifully.***	Das Lied ist **schön.** *The song is **beautiful.***
Du hast das **gut** gemacht. *You did that **well.***	Dieses Buch ist **gut.** *This book is **good.***

German, like English, also has words which can function only as adverbs.

Das Haus ist **sehr** groß.
*The house is **very** big.*

Er kommt **bald.**
*He is coming **soon.***

< < What is a Preposition? > >

A **preposition** is a word which shows the relationship between a noun or pronoun and another word in the sentence. Prepositions may indicate position, direction or time.

In English: Here are examples of some prepositions:

- to show position

  Bob was ***in*** the car.
  She is sitting ***behind*** you.

- to show direction

  Mary went ***to*** school.
  The students came directly ***from*** class.

- to show time

  German people go on vacation ***in*** August.
  Their son will be home ***at*** Christmas.

- to show manner

  They left ***without*** us.
  He writes ***with*** a pen.

The noun or pronoun which the preposition connects to the rest of the sentence is called the **object of the preposition**. The preposition and its object together make up a **prepositional phrase**.

In German: You will have to memorize prepositions as vocabulary items. In German all prepositions take objects in a particular case (accusative, dative, or genitive). When you learn a preposition, you will have to learn which case it requires for its object. Below there are examples of prepositions which take

- an accusative object

Der Hund läuft **durch die Tür.**

feminine singular accusative
Durch always requires an accusative object.

The dog is running ***through the door.***

Sie kauft etwas **für ihren Bruder.**

masculine singular accusative
Für always requires an accusative object.

She is buying something ***for her brother.***

Wir fahren morgen **in die Stadt.**

feminine singular accusative
In requires an accusative object when used with verbs expressing movement in one direction.

We are going ***into town*** *tomorrow.*

- a dative object

Er wohnt **bei seiner Tante.**

feminine singular dative
Bei always requires a dative object.

He lives ***with his aunt.***

Fahren Sie **mit dem Wagen?**

masculine singular dative
Mit always requires a dative object.

Are you going ***by car?***

Wohnt ihr **in der Stadt?**

feminine singular dative
In requires a dative object when used with verbs which do not express movement in one direction.

*Do you live **in the city**?*

- a genitive object

Trotz des Regens machten wir einen Spaziergang.

masculine singular genitive
Trotz always requires a genitive object.

***In spite of the rain** we took a walk.*

Wegen der Kälte ziehe ich mir den Wintermantel an.

feminine singular genitive
Wegen always requires a genitive object.

***On account of the cold** I'm putting on my winter coat.*

German also has a group of prepositions called **two-way prepositions**. These prepositions can take either an accusative object or a dative object: 1. a dative object when they are used with a verb expressing no directed motion 2. an accusative object when they are used with a verb expressing motion in a particular direction.

an *She is standing **at the window**.*
Sie steht **am Fenster**.

dative object
to stand implies no directed motion

*She walks up **to the window**.*
Sie geht **ans Fenster**.

accusative object
to walk implies directed motion

auf *He lays the book* ***on the table.***
Er legt das Buch **auf den Tisch**.
accusative object
to lay implies directed motion

The book lies ***on the table.***
Das Buch liegt **auf dem Tisch**.
dative object
to lie implies no directed motion

In learning how to use German prepositions, there are two important things to remember:

1. Prepositions are tricky little words. Every language uses prepositions differently. Do not assume that the same preposition is used in German as in English, or that one is even used at all.

English	German
preposition → no preposition	
to look *for*	suchen
to look *at*	betrachten
no preposition → preposition	
to answer	antworten **auf**
change of preposition	
to protect *from*	schützen **vor** (*before*)
to wait *for*	warten **auf** (*on*)
to die *of*	sterben **an** (*at*)

2. The position of a preposition in an English sentence is much more variable than in a German sentence. Spoken English tends to place the preposition at the end of the sentence far from its object; this is called a **dangling preposition**. Formal English places the preposition within the sentence or at the beginning of a question. Look at the position of the preposition in the following sentences:

Spoken English		Formal English
Here is the man I speak *to.*	→	Here is the man *to whom* I speak.
Who(m) are you playing *with*?	→	*With whom* are you playing?
That's the teacher I'm talking *about.*	→	That's the teacher *about whom* I'm talking.

The position of a preposition in a German sentence is the same as in formal English; that is, it is never at the end of a sentence. Nearly all German prepositions immediately precede their objects (a few must or can directly follow their objects); none, however, can be separated from its object and moved to another part of the sentence. When expressing an English sentence in German remember to restructure dangling prepositions: it will enable you to find the object of the preposition and will correspond to German sentence structure. (See p. 24.)

Look at the above English sentences when they are translated into German:

- *Here is the man I speak to.*

Here is the man I speak *to.* → Here is the man *to whom* I speak.

Hier ist der Mann, **mit dem** ich rede.

- *Who are you playing with?*

Who are you playing *with*?	→ *With whom* are you playing?

Mit wem spielst du?

- *That is the teacher I am talking about.*

That is the teacher I am talking *about*.	→ That is the teacher *about whom* I am talking.

Das ist der Lehrer, **von dem** ich rede.

It is important that you remember that German prepositions are never separated from their object, because you will often see German sentences which look as though they end in a preposition:

Wer kommt **mit**?	*Who is coming along?*
Das kommt machmal **vor**.	*That happens sometimes.*
Der Zug hält in München **an**.	*The train stops in Munich.*

Mit, **vor** and **an** all look like prepositions. However, in the above three sentences, they are all really separable prefixes of verbs (see **What are Prefixes and Suffixes?**, p. 136).

mitkommen	*to come along*
vorkommen	*to happen*
anhalten	*to stop*

If you remember that a preposition cannot come at the end of a German sentence, you will recognize **mit**, **vor**, and **an** as part of the verb. Only when you realize that the prefix and the verb belong together can you understand the sentence properly.

< < What are Prefixes and Suffixes? > >

A **prefix** is one or more syllables added to the beginning of a word to change that word's meaning.

nuclear	*anti*nuclear
believe	*dis*believe

A **suffix** is one or more syllables added to the end of a word to change that word's part of speech.

gentle	gentle*ness*
love	love*able*

For an example of how prefixes and suffixes work, let us look at the various different English words which come from the Latin verb **duco** (*to lead*). Different prefixes give us the verbs ***in**duce*, ***re**duce*, ***se**duce*, ***pro**duce*, ***intro**duce*, ***ad**duce*, ***e**duce*. With different suffixes we can change these verbs into other parts of speech: *induc**tion*** (noun), *induc**tive*** (adjective), *induc**tively*** (adverb).

In English: Most of our prefixes and suffixes come from Latin and Greek. Knowing the meaning of prefixes can help you increase your English vocabulary.[1]

For example:

anti- (against)	+	body	= *anti*body
sub- (under)	+	marine	= *sub*marine
mal- (bad)	+	nutrition	= *mal*nutrition

[1] For a good list of such prefixes and suffixes, see Sheridan Baker, **The Complete Stylist and Handbook** (New York: Thomas Y. Crowell, 1976), pp. 180-181.

Likewise, knowing English suffixes can help you identify the parts of speech in a sentence.

For example:

-able/-ible	toler*able*	→	adjective
-ence/-ance	reli*ance*	→	noun
-or	debt*or*	→	noun

In German: Prefixes and suffixes can communicate even more information than they do in English. Let us look at how they affect the nouns and verbs to which they can be attached.

A. Prefixes and suffixes used with nouns

Certain suffixes not only affect the meaning of the noun but also determine the gender of the noun.

-chen and **-lein** — Diminutive suffixes showing that the stem noun has been reduced in size.

Gender: The noun will be neuter.

Stem noun		New noun	
das Brot	*bread*	das Böt**chen**	*roll, little bread*
das Buch	*book*	das Büch**lein**	*booklet*
die Frau	*woman*	das Fräu**lein**	*young woman, miss*

-heit and **-keit** — Suffixes which make an adjective into a noun expressing an abstract quality.

Gender: The noun will be feminine.

Stem adjective		New noun	
schön	*beautiful*	die Schön**heit**	*beauty*
frei	*free*	die Frei**heit**	*freedom*
möglich	*possible*	die Möglich**keit**	*possibility*

B. Prefixes used with verbs

These are very versatile and function very differently from English prefixes. Verb prefixes are divided into two groups:

1. **Separable prefixes**—those prefixes that can be detached from the verb.
2. **Inseparable prefixes**—those prefixes that cannot be detached from the verb.

We shall consider each type separately below.

1. Separable prefixes—The most common separable prefixes in German are the following:

ab	nach
an	vor
auf	weiter
aus	zu
ein	zurück
mit	

- These prefixes are detached from the verb in the present or simple past tense of a main clause:

Infinitive

ausgehen *to go out* — Hans und ich **gehen** morgen **aus**. (present tense)

*Hans and I **are going out** tomorrow.*

ankommen *to arrive* — Der Zug **kam** spät **an**. (simple past tense)

*The train **arrived** late.*

- In the perfect tenses, the **ge-** prefix of the past participle is inserted between the separable prefix and the verb stem:

Hans und ich **sind** gestern **ausgegangen.**

auxiliary verb — **aus** = separable prefix; **ge** = prefix of past participle; **gangen** = verb stem in past participle

*Hans and I **went out** yesterday.*

Der Zug **war** sehr spät **angekommen.**

auxiliary verb — **an** = separable prefix; **ge** = prefix of past participle; **kommen** = verb stem in past participle

*The train **had arrived** late.*

- In a subordinate or dependent clause (see **What are Subordinate or Dependent Clauses?**, p. 157), the separable prefix is reunited with the verb stem:

Ich höre, daß ihr morgen **ausgeht.**

prefix + verb together at end of subordinate clause

*I hear you **are going out** tomorrow.*

Ich hoffe, daß der Zug nicht zu spät **ankommt.**

prefix + verb together at end of subordinate clause

*I hope that the train doesn't **arrive** too late.*

2. Inseparable prefixes–The most common inseparable prefixes are the following:

be-	ge-
emp-	ver-
ent-	zer-
er-	

- These function more like verb prefixes in English in that they are never separated from their stem verb.

Wir **be**suchen unsere Tante.
We're visiting our aunt.

Er **be**kam gestern einen Brief.
He received a letter yesterday.

Du **ver**gißt immer dein Buch.
You always forget your book.

- In the perfect tenses, the verbs with these inseparable prefixes do not have a **ge-** in the past participle.

Peter hat uns **be**sucht.
auxiliary verb (hat) — past participle (besucht)

Peter visited us.

Ilse hatte die Telefonnummer **ver**loren.
auxiliary verb (hatte) — past participle (verloren)

Ilse had lost the telephone number.

These two kinds of verb prefixes also affect the way the verbs are pronounced.

The separable prefixes are always accented:

ankommen
einsteigen
abfahren
mitnehmen

The inseparable prefixes are always unaccented:

besuchen
erfahren
verlieren
zerfallen

The addition of a separable or inseparable prefix to a verb has no effect on the conjugation of that verb. Both groups of verbs include both strong and weak verbs (see **What are the Principal Parts of a Verb?**, p. 46). Your German textbook will provide you with many more examples of these verbs and their uses.

< < What is Meant by Active and Passive Voice? > >

Active voice and passive voice are terms used to describe the relationship between the verb and its subject.

In English: The **active voice** of a verb expresses an action performed by the subject.

The woman reads the novel.
subject verb direct object

The boy is closing the window.
subject verb direct object

The medicine healed the patient.
subject verb direct object

In all these examples the subject performs the action of the verb and the direct object receives the action of the verb.

The **passive voice** of a verb expresses an action performed on the subject. The passive voice in English is expressed by the verb *to be*, conjugated in the proper tense, **+ the past participle of the main verb.**

The novel *is read* by the woman.
subject verb agent

The window *is being closed* by the boy.
subject verb agent

The patient *was healed* by the medicine.
subject verb agent

In all these examples the subject is not performing the action but is receiving the action of the verb. Note that verbs in the passive voice can be in all the different tenses; the tense of the auxiliary ***to be*** indicates the tense of the whole verb.

The novel *is* read by the woman.
present passive

The novel *was* read by the woman.
past passive

The novel *has been* read by the woman.
present perfect passive

In English only **transitive verbs** (verbs having a direct object) can be used in the passive voice.

Active: Many people saw the film.
subject (people) — transitive verb (saw) — direct object (film)

Passive: The film was seen by many people.
subject (formerly direct object) (film) — verb (was seen) — agent (people)

Active: The mechanic is repairing the car.
subject (mechanic) — transitive verb (is repairing) — direct object (car)

Passive: The car is being repaired by the mechanic.
subject (formerly direct object) (car) — verb (is being repaired) — agent (mechanic)

Note that when an active sentence is changed into a passive one the following occurs:

1. The direct object of the active sentence becomes the subject of the passive sentence.
2. The subject of the active sentence becomes the agent of the passive sentence (although the agent is often omitted).

In German: The passive voice is formed by the verb *werden*, conjugated in the proper tense, **+ the past participle of the main verb**.

- The tense of passive sentences is shown by the tense of the verb **werden**; verbs in the passive voice can be in all the different tenses.

Der Roman **wird** gelesen.
present
The novel ***is (being)*** *read.*

Der Roman **wurde** gelesen.
simple past
The novel ***was (being)*** *read.*

Der Roman **ist** gelesen **worden**.
perfect
The novel ***was (has been)*** *read.*

Der Roman **war** gelesen **worden**.
pluperfect
The novel ***had been*** *read.*

NOTE: In the perfect and pluperfect passive a contracted form is used for the past participle of **werden**:

geworden → worden

- When you change an active sentence to a passive sentence, you must also remember to use the proper cases for subject and agent and make sure the verb agrees in number with the new subject.

1. The accusative object (**AO**) of an active sentence becomes the subject (**S**) of the passive sentence; its case changes from accusative to nominative.

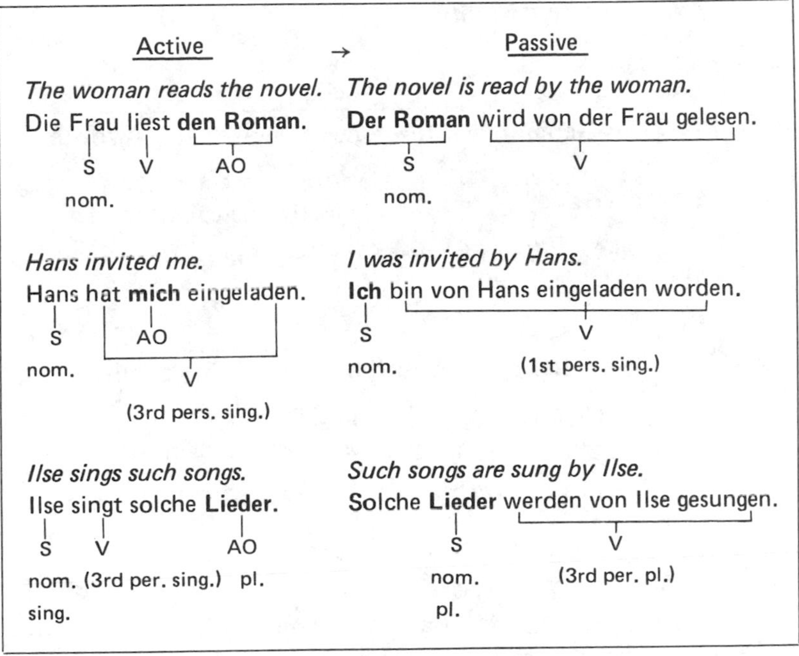

2. If the agent of a passive sentence is a person, it is expressed by *von* + **a dative object**:

verb

Die Rede wurde **von vielen Menschen** gehört.

subject — agent, dative plural

The speech was heard ***by many people***.

verb

Dieses Haus wird **von meiner Schwester** gebaut.

subject — agent, dative feminine singular

This house is being built ***by my sister.***

3. If the agent is not a person, it is usually expressed by *durch* + **accusative object**:

verb

Das Gebäude ist **durch das Feuer** zerstört worden.

subject — impersonal agent, accusative masculine singular

The building was destroyed ***by the fire.***

verb

Der Patient wurde **durch die Medizin** geheilt.

subject — impersonal agent, accusative feminine singular

The patient was healed ***by the medicine.***

4. If you change a sentence which has only a dative object from active to passive, the dative object does not become the nominative subject of the new sentence. Instead, it remains in the dative case.

Active: Man dankt **ihm.**

subject verb dative object

One thanks ***him.***

Passive: **Ihm** wird gedankt.

He *is thanked.*

<u>Active</u>: Sie glaubten **den Kindern** nicht.
subject verb dative object
*They didn't believe **the children**.*

<u>Passive</u>: **Den Kindern** wurde nicht geglaubt.
***The children** were not believed.*

NOTE: These passive sentences have no grammatical subject. The verb will always be singular.

- German, unlike English, sometimes uses intransitive verbs (verbs without an object) in the passive voice. These verbs express activity as such without any specified agent and are called impersonal passives. The construction cannot be translated adequately into English.

Samstags wird hier getanzt.
adverb passive verb
There is dancing here on Saturdays.

Jetzt wird hier gearbeitet.
adverb passive verb
Work is being done here now.

These sentences have no grammatical subject.

Your German textbook will show you several alternative constructions with which to express passive sentences in German.

<< What is a Conjunction? >>

A **conjunction** is a word which joins words, phrases, or clauses (see **What is a Sentence?**, p. 151).

> Paul plays basketball *and* tennis.
> We are going over the river *and* through the woods.
> I liked *neither* the book *nor* the play.
> The children are happy *whenever* he comes.

There are two kinds of conjunctions: co-ordinating and subordinating.

1. **Co-ordinating conjunctions** join words, phrases, and clauses that are equal; they *co-ordinate* things of equal rank.

> good *or* evil
> over the river *and* through the woods
> They invited us, *but* we couldn't come.

2. **Subordinating conjunctions** join a clause to the main clause; they *subordinate* one thought to another one.

Clauses introduced by a subordinating conjunction are called subordinate clauses. (See p. 157.)

Although we were invited, we didn't go.
Although = subordinating conjunction; we didn't go = main clause

They left *because* they were bored.
They left = main clause; *because* = subordinating conjunction

He said *that* he was tired.
He said = main clause; *that* = subordinating conjunction

Notice that the main clause is not always the first clause of the sentence.

In English: The major co-ordinating conjunctions are ***and***, ***but***, ***or***, ***nor***, and ***for***. Typical subordinating conjunctions are ***although***, ***because***, ***if***, ***unless***, ***so that***, ***while***, ***that***, and ***whenever***. Some words exist as both prepositions and subordinating conjunctions.

We can distinguish between a preposition and a subordinating conjunction simply by determining if the word over which we are hesitating introduces a clause or not: if it does, the word is a subordinating conjunction, if it does not, it is a preposition. Look at the two following examples where the same word is used as a preposition and as a subordinating conjunction:

- We left *before* the intermission.
  - *before* — preposition
  - *intermission* — object of preposition

  We left *before* the intermission began.
  - *before* — subordinating conjunction
  - *before the intermission began* — clause
  - *intermission began* — subject + verb

- *After* the concert we ate ice cream.
  - *After* — preposition
  - *concert* — object of preposition

  After the concert was over, we ate ice cream.
  - *After* — subordinating conjunction
  - *After the concert was over* — clause
  - *concert was* — subject + verb

In German: Conjunctions are to be memorized as vocabulary items. Remember that like adverbs and prepositions, conjunctions are invariable; they never change. (They never become plural, nor do they have a case or gender.)

The major co-ordinating conjunctions are **und** (*and*), **oder** (*or*), **aber** (*but*), **sondern** (*but=on the contrary*), and **denn** (*for*). Typical subordinating conjunctions are **obgleich** (*although*), **obwohl** (*although*), **weil** (*because*), **wenn** (*if, whenever*), **damit** (*in order that*), **daß** (*that*), and **während** (*while*).

You cannot assume that a word which serves as both preposition and conjunction in English also serves as both in German.

- *We left* ***before*** *the intermission.*
  Wir sind **vor** der Pause weggegangen.
  preposition — object of preposition

  We left ***before*** *the intermission began.*
  Wir sind weggegangen, **bevor** die Pause anfing.
  subordinating conjunction — subject + verb

- ***After*** *the concert we ate ice cream.*
  Nach dem Konzert haben wir Eis gegessen.
  preposition — object of preposition

  After *the concert was over, we ate ice cream.*
  Nachdem das Konzert vorbei war, haben wir Eis gegessen.
  subordinating conjunction — subject + verb

These examples show you how important it is that you understand the difference between a conjunction and a preposition and that you learn the part of speech of each vocabulary word you memorize.

< < What are Sentences, Phrases and Clauses? > >

What is a sentence?

A **sentence** is the expression of a thought consisting at the very least of a subject (see **What is a Subject?**, p. 18) and a verb (see **What is a Verb?**, p. 44).

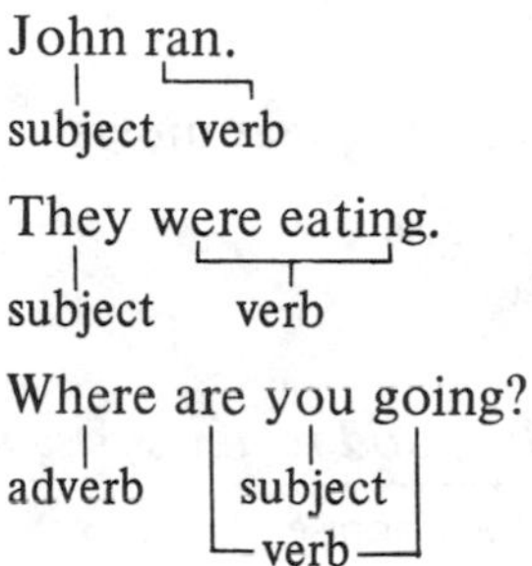

Depending on the verb, a sentence may also have direct and indirect objects (see **What are Objects?**, p. 20).

She reads the book.
subject verb direct object

They gave him a present.
subject verb indirect object direct object

In addition, a sentence may include various kinds of modifiers: adjectives (see **What is an Adjective?**, p. 115), adverbs (see **What is an Adverb?**, p. 127), prepositional phrases (see **What is a Preposition?**, p. 130), participial phrases (see **What is a Participle?**, p. 62).

I saw a movie.
subject verb object

I saw a *great* movie.
adjective

Yesterday I saw a great movie.
adverb

Yesterday *after work* I saw a great movie.
prepositional phrase modifying *saw*

Yesterday, *attracted by good reviews*, I saw a great movie.
participial phrase modifying *I*

Although not all of these elements of a sentence occur in German in the same way that they do in English, you will find it very helpful to recognize all the different parts of a sentence in each language. Moreover, it will be important for you to recognize complete sentences and to distinguish phrases and clauses from complete sentences.

What is a phrase?

A **phrase** is simply a group of words in a sentence which belong together on the basis of their meaning. A phrase may contain an object, but it does not have both a subject and a conjugated verb. The various phrases are identified by the type of word beginning the phrase.

- **Prepositional phrase**: starts with a *preposition*

through the door
preposition — object of preposition

after the concert
preposition — object of preposition

- **Participial phrase**: starts with a *participle*

leaving the room
present participle of *to leave* — object of *leaving*

pasted on the wall
past participle of *to paste* — prepositional phrase used, adverbially, to modify *pasted*

- **Infinitive phrase**: starts with an *infinitive*

to learn German
infinitive — object of *to learn*

to read intelligently
infinitive — adverb modifying *to read*

To recognize such phrases you need to recognize the individual parts (prepositions, participles, infinitives) and then isolate all those words within a group of words which work as one block of meaning. If this block of meaning does not have both a subject and a conjugated verb, it is a phrase.

What is a clause?

A **clause** is a part of a sentence which itself has its own subject and conjugated verb.

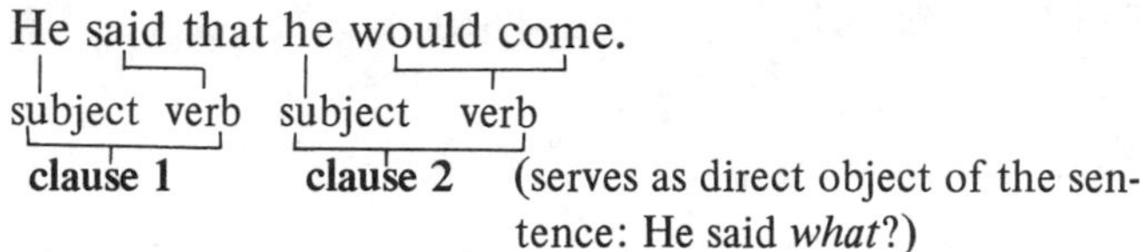

You can distinguish each of these clauses from a phrase by the presence of a subject and a conjugated verb in each one. You can distinguish each of them from a complete sentence if you try to use them separately. Neither "he said" nor "that he would come" expresses a finished thought; therefore neither is a complete sentence. Instead, both are parts of a whole sentence.

Let us look at the various types of sentences:

A. A **simple sentence** is a sentence consisting of only one clause.

In English: There is no set position for the verb in an English sentence or clause; but the subject almost always comes before the verb.

We went to the concert.
subject verb

Some other modifier can come before the subject.

Yesterday we went to a concert.
adverb

After the party we went to a concert.
prepositional phrase modifying *went*

In German: In a simple declarative sentence (a statement), the conjugated verb always stands in second position. This does not mean that the verb is always the second word in the sentence: it means that if the sentence begins with some modifier (an adverb or a prepositional phrase, for example), the verb must come immediately second. Compare the structure of the German sentences with that of the English ones:

- Wir **gingen** in ein Konzert.
  subject verb
  1st position 2nd position
  we *went* to a concert

- Gestern **gingen** wir in ein Konzert.
  adverb verb subject
  1st position 2nd position
  yesterday *went* we to a concert

- Nach der Party **gingen** wir in ein Konzert.
  prepositional phrase verb subject
  1st position 2nd position
  after the party *went* we to a concert

- Spät gestern abend nach der Party **gingen** wir in ein Konzert.

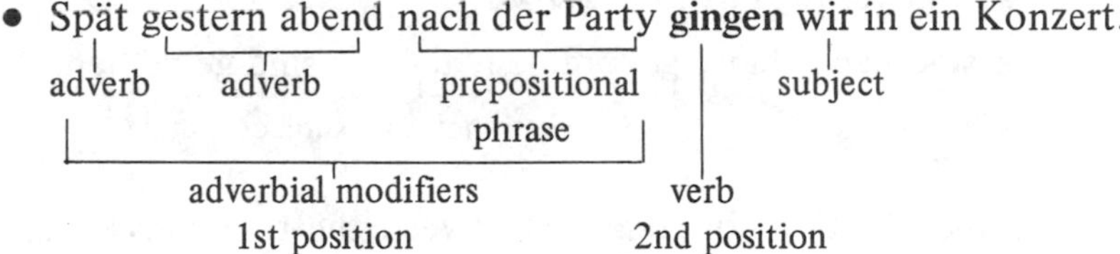

late yesterday evening after the party *went* we to a concert

Only in the first example is it possible to put the subject before the verb in the German sentence. In sentences 2,3, and 4 that space is already occupied by a modifier; the verb must come second, and the subject then must follow the verb.

B. A **compound sentence** consists of two statements or equal clauses. These two statements are joined by co-ordinating conjunctions (see **What is a Conjunction?**, p. 148). In both English and German the word order is the same as for any simple sentence.

In English: Remember that the position of the verb can vary in a simple sentence.

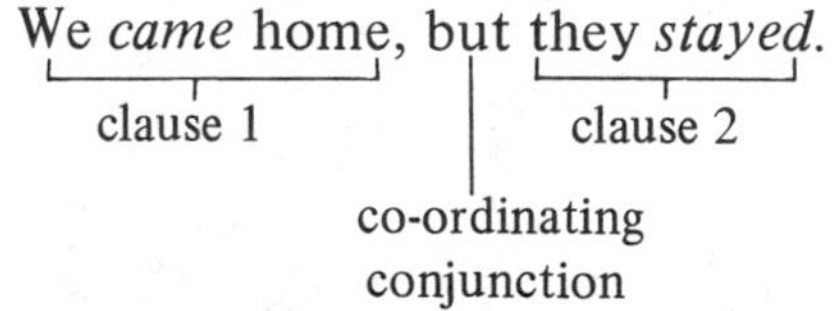

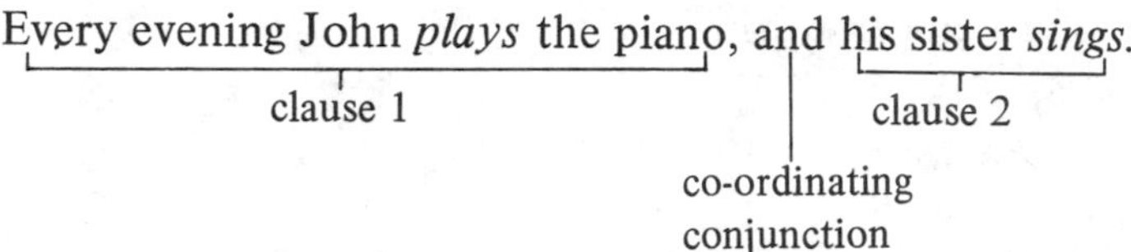

In German: It is important that you know how to recognize a compound sentence. Usually the two statements of a compound sentence are both simple sentences. This means that in German each of them will have the conjugated verb in second position:

We came home, but they stayed.

Wir sind nach Hause gekommen, aber sie sind geblieben.

subject (Wir) verb (sind) — conjunction (aber) subject (sie) verb (sind geblieben)

The co-ordinating conjunction between the two clauses has no effect on the word order of the second clause.

C. A **complex sentence** is a sentence consisting of a main clause and one or more subordinate clauses:

The **main clause** (or independent clause) in a complex sentence could stand alone as a complete sentence.

The **subordinate clause** (or dependent clause) cannot stand alone as a complete sentence; it depends on the main clause for its full meaning, and it is subordinate to the main clause.

Although it was raining, we took a walk.
subordinate clause — main clause

It makes sense to say "we took a walk" without the first clause in the sentence; therefore, it is a main clause. It does not make sense to say simply, "although it was raining" unless we add a conclusion; therefore, it is a subordinate clause.

In English: It is important that you be able to distinguish a main clause from a subordinate clause. This will help you to write complete sentences and avoid sentence fragments.

In German: The distinction between the main clause and the subordinate clause is much more important than in English because each kind of clause has its own word order.

In the main clause the position of the verb will remain the same as in a simple sentence; that is, the verb will be in second position. This structure can be very different from that of an English sentence.

Although it was raining, we took a walk.
subordinate clause 1st position — subject 2nd position — verb 3rd position

Obwohl es regnete, machten wir einen Spaziergang.
subordinate clause 1st position — verb 2nd position — subject 3rd position

In the subordinate clause, the conjugated verb stands at the end, except in a few special constructions.

Although it was beginning to rain, . . .

subordinating conjunction — subject — verb

Obwohl es zu regnen anfing, . . .

subordinating conjunction — subject — verb

Your German textbook will explain this structure in more detail. The important thing is that you be able to recognize a subordinate clause when you see one.

<< Appendix A - Noun Gender Reference List >>

1. Masculine **(maskulin)**

- Nouns referring to persons which end in **-er**, **-ist**, **-ling**, **-ent**. Plural formed by adding **--**, **-e** or **-en**.

der Physiker	→	die Physiker
der Jüngling	→	die Jünglinge
der Pianist	→	die Pianisten
der Referent	→	die Referenten

A more general rule: nouns referring to human beings are masculine unless they specifically refer to feminine humans (which then have feminine gender). Be careful, however, with diminutives **(das Fräulein, das Mädchen)**, which are covered in 3.

- Names of seasons, months, days and parts of days (except **die Nacht**).

der Sommer
der Januar
der Montag
der Mittag

NOTE: **das Frühjahr**, another term for **der Frühling**, is neuter because **Jahr** is neuter.

- Nouns which end in:

-g (but not **-ung**) der Tag
-en (but not **-chen** or gerunds) der Rücken
-f der Senf
-tz der Blitz

- Most one-syllable nouns made from verbs.

der Schritt
der Sitz
der Gang

2. Feminine **(feminin)**

- Most 2-syllable nouns which end in **-e**.
  Plural formed by adding **-n**.

die Lampe	→	die Lampen
die Seife	→	die Seifen

(Some common exceptions are: **der Name, der Käse, das Auge.**)

- Nouns referring to female human beings which end in **-in**.
  Plural formed by adding **-nen**.

die Studentin	→	die Studentinnen
die Professorin	→	die Professorinnen

- Nouns which end in:

-erei	die Bücherei	→	die Büchereien
-ie	die Drogerie	→	die Drogerien
-heit	die Dummheit	→	die Dummheiten
-keit	die Möglichkeit	→	die Möglichkeiten
-schaft	die Mannschaft	→	die Mannschaften
-ung	die Prüfung	→	die Prüfungen
-ion	die Reaktion	→	die Reaktionen
-tät	die Universität	→	die Universitäten
-ade	die Fassade	→	die Fassaden
-ik	die Musik		
-ur	die Natur		
-unft	die Vernunft		
-enz	die Lizenz	→	die Lizenzen

3. Neuter **(neutral)**

- Nouns ending in the diminutive suffixes **-lein** or **-chen**.
  Plural just like singular.

das Mädchen	→	die Mädchen
das Büchlein	→	die Büchlein
das Fräulein	→	die Fräulein

- Verb infinitives used as nouns (gerunds).
  No plural possible.

  das Lesen
  das Essen
  das Singen

- Nouns which end in **-um**.
  Plural with **⸚ er.**

  das Bistum → die Bistümer

- Most nouns which end in **-nis**.
  Plural with **-se**.

  das Hindernis → die Hindernisse

<< Index >>